*The Report of the President's Commission
on an All-Volunteer Armed Force*

The Report of the President's Commission on an All-Volunteer Armed Force

Generously Donated to
The Frederick Douglass Institute
y Professor Jesse Moore
Fall 2000

COLLIER BOOKS/THE MACMILLAN COMPANY
COLLIER-MACMILLAN LTD., LONDON

PRESIDENT'S COMMISSION
ON AN ALL-VOLUNTEER ARMED FORCE
726 *Jackson Pl., N.W.*
Washington, D.C. 20506

February 20, 1970

Dear Mr. President:

The report of your Commission on an All-Volunteer Armed Force is submitted herewith.

We unanimously believe that the nation's interests will be better served by an all-volunteer force, supported by an effective standby draft, than by a mixed force of volunteers and conscripts; that steps should be taken promptly to move in this direction; and that the first indispensable step is to remove the present inequity in the pay of men serving their first term in the armed forces.

We have satisfied ourselves that a volunteer force will not jeopardize national security, and we believe it will have a beneficial effect on the military as well as the rest of our society.

The findings and recommendations summarized in Part I are unanimously agreed to. These are based on the detailed discussion in Part II, Chapters 3 through 15.

The President created the Commission on March 27, 1969. A working staff was assembled promptly under the direction of Dean William H. Meckling of the University of Rochester, and the Commission first met on May 15, 1969.

The members of the Commission began their work with different views, based on their own diverse experiences. They represent a wide cross section of age, race, sex, religion, political affiliation, and occupation. It is somewhat remarkable that, starting from different backgrounds and opinions, they concluded the report in agreement.

This came about as the result of numerous official meetings, totaling more than 100 hours, usually over weekends in Washington. In addition, Commission members worked diligently on their own time in order to review the hundreds of pages of staff memoranda devoted to the study and review of this vital subject.

One member, Mr. Roy Wilkins, was unable to participate in much of the Commission's later deliberations because of ill health, and, for this reason, has not signed the report. A letter from Mr. Wilkins to this effect is enclosed.

We consulted a wide range of representatives of the public, interested organizations, and experts as well as the Service Secretaries, the Joint Chiefs of Staff and other high officials in the Department of Defense and armed forces. We appreciate greatly their cooperation and valuable contributions.

Members of our staff came from academic life, the military, and business. The full extent of their efforts will be reflected in a companion volume of technical studies being prepared for publication next summer. We are very grateful for the quality of their work as well as their dedication, exemplified by their unhesitating willingness to work long hours to complete this report. I particularly want to thank the Executive Director of the staff, William Meckling.

It has been a remarkable experience and education, and the Commission thanks you for the opportunity to advise you.

We hope the report serves not only your needs, but those of Congress and the public.

With great respect,

Thomas Gates

THOMAS S. GATES

February 6, 1970

Dear Mr. President:

It was an honor to be named by you to membership on the President's Commission on an All-Volunteer Armed Force. I looked forward to serving on this Commission because it confronts an extremely important issue. Unfortunately, a combination of a minor illness in December and an operation at the beginning of January prevented my participating in the last five Commission meetings during which specific recommendations and various drafts of the report were discussed.

Because I was able to play only a small part in its shaping I did not feel it was proper for me to sign the report, and advised the Chairman, Thomas Gates, accordingly in late December.

I am writing now to express my regret at not being able to sign this report. Although I have been unable to share in its specific recommendations, I would like to endorse the basic idea of moving towards an all-volunteer armed force, and to express my hope that you will be able to take steps in the near future to reduce reliance on conscription.

Respectfully,

Roy Wilkins

ROY WILKINS

The Honorable RICHARD M. NIXON
The White House
Washington, D.C.

STATEMENT BY THE PRESIDENT
ANNOUNCING THE CREATION
OF THE COMMISSION

To achieve the goal of an all-volunteer force we will require the best efforts of our military establishment and the best advice we can obtain from eminent citizens and experts in many related fields of national endeavor. For this purpose, I have today appointed an Advisory Commission on an All-Volunteer Armed Force under the Chairmanship of the Honorable Thomas S. Gates, Jr., former Secretary of Defense.

I have directed the Commission to develop a comprehensive plan for eliminating conscription and moving toward an all-volunteer armed force. The Commission will study a broad range of possibilities for increasing the supply of volunteers for service, including increased pay, benefits, recruitment incentives and other practicable measures to make military careers more attractive to young men. It will consider possible changes in selection standards and in utilization policies which may assist in eliminating the need for inductions. It will study the estimated costs and savings resulting from an all-volunteer force, as well as the broader social and economic implications of this program.

The transition to an all-volunteer armed force must, of course, be handled cautiously and responsibly so that our national security is fully maintained. The Commission will determine what standby machinery for the draft will be required in the event of a national emergency and will give serious consideration to our requirements for an adequate reserve forces program.

I have instructed the Department of Defense and other agencies of the Executive Branch to support this study and provide needed information and assistance as a matter of high priority.

PRESIDENT'S COMMISSION
ON AN ALL-VOLUNTEER ARMED FORCE

THOMAS GATES CHAIRMAN	Chairman of the Executive Committee of Morgan Guaranty Trust Co. Former Secretary of Defense. New York City
THOMAS CURTIS	Vice-President and General Counsel, Encyclopedia Britannica. Former Congressman from Missouri and ranking Republican on Joint Economic Committee, United States Congress. St. Louis, Missouri
FREDERICK DENT	President, Mayfair Mills. Spartanburg, South Carolina
MILTON FRIEDMAN	Paul Snowdon Russell Distinguished Service Professor of Economics, University of Chicago. Chicago, Illinois
CRAWFORD GREENEWALT	Chairman, Finance Committee, E. I. duPont de Nemours and Co. Wilmington, Delaware
ALAN GREENSPAN	Chairman of the Board, Townsend-Greenspan & Co. Economic consultants. New York City
ALFRED GRUENTHER	Former Supreme Allied Commander, Europe. Washington, D. C.
STEPHEN HERBITS	Student, Georgetown University Law Center. Washington, D. C.
THEODORE HESBURGH	President, University of Notre Dame. Chairman, U.S. Commission on Civil Rights. South Bend, Indiana
JEROME HOLLAND	President, Hampton Institute. Hampton, Virginia

COMMISSION STAFF

Executive Director
William H. Meckling

Directors of Research
Dr. Stuart Altman
Dr. Harry J. Gilman
David Kassing
Dr. Walter Y. Oi

Deputy Executive Director
David J. Callard

Editor
Richard J. Whalen

Research Projects

Lt. Col. Ames Albro *(U.S. Army)—Potential for Civilian Substitution*
Robert Barro—*Officer Recruitment*
Lt. Col. Herman Boland *(U.S. Army)—Reserve Requirements and Supply*
Dr. Alvin Cook—*Air Force Enlistments*
Alan Fechter—*Army Enlistments*
Brian Forst—*Personnel Requirements*
Burton Gray—*Navy Enlistments*
Dr. Harry Grubert—*Navy Reenlistments*
Ronald N. Hansen—*The Conscription Tax*
Stewart Kemp—*Recruiting Practices*
Mordechai Lando—*Conscription of Physicians*
James McConnell—*Conscription in Europe*

J. Houston McCulloch—*Civilian Earnings*
Gary Nelson—*Army Reenlistments*
Dr. Dave M. O'Neil—*Costs of Military Personnel Turnover*
John L. Rafuse—*Conscription in America*
Dave Reaume—*Utilization of Skills by the Armed Forces*
Dr. Larry Sjaastad—*The Conscription Tax*
David Stigler—*Conscription and the Constitution*
John Sullivan—*Qualitative Requirements of Enlisted Men*
Dr. Rodney Weiher—*Navy Reenlistments*
Dr. Robert White—*Air Force Enlistments*
Capt. Robert Wilburn *(U.S. Air Force)—Air Force Reenlistments*
Dr. Desmond P. Wilson—*Veterans in Society*

Research Assistants

Judith Blaine
Mary Clark
Patricia Flanary
Eleanor Garges
William Holahan

Jesse Horack
Andrea Hornett
Ruth Kurtz
Joanne Linnerooth
Mary Ostrander

Data Processing

James Parsells   Sheila Rafferty

Office Staff

Dimitrios Drivas   Robin D. Margenau
Candy Haga   Warren Parker
Dorothy Hitselberger   Marty Roberts
Rose Lawrence   Allaire Williams

Consulting Organizations

Center for Naval Analyses
Institute for Defense Analysis
Rand Corporation

Contents

Introduction

The Commission's report consists of two parts—the first, Chapters 1 and 2; and the second, Chapters 3 through 15.

In Chapter 1 we take up the questions we recognized as critical from the outset. Is an all-volunteer force feasible? Are there practicable reforms in present procedures that will maintain voluntary forces of the size and quality deemed necessary for national security? Chapter 1 summarizes the considerations underlying our conclusion that an all-volunteer force is feasible and lists our recommendations for major reforms.

Chapter 2 deals with another set of questions. Regardless of whether an all-volunteer force is feasible, is it desirable? Will voluntary recruitment weaken our democratic society and have harmful political and social effects? The Commission has studied such issues at great length, in the light of whatever relevant evidence we could assemble. Chapter 2 notes some of the main objections raised to ending conscription and summarizes our responses to them.

In Part II of the report, the Commission presents the pertinent evidence gathered during its inquiry and the analysis underlying its recommendations which form the essential background to the Commission's findings.

Of course, the members of the Commission in expressing their individual views on this broad range of issues, would choose a variety of phrases to express their particular emphases and therefore should not be held individually responsible for each and every sentence of the report.

PART I

CHAPTER 1

Protecting the Free Society

Since the founding of the republic, a primary task of the government of the United States has been to provide for the common defense of a society established to secure the blessings of liberty and justice. Without endangering the nation's security, the means of defense should support the aims of the society.

The armed forces today play an honorable and important part in promoting the nation's security, as they have since our freedoms were won on the battlefield at Yorktown. A fundamental consideration that has guided this Commission is the need to maintain and improve the effectiveness, dignity, and status of the armed forces so they may continue to play their proper role.

The Commission has not attempted to judge the size of the armed forces the nation requires. Instead, it has accepted a range of estimates made for planning purposes which anticipate maintaining a total force in the future somewhere between 2,000,000 and 3,000,000 men.

We unanimously believe that the nation's interests will be better served by an all-volunteer force, supported by an effective standby draft, than by a mixed force of volunteers and conscripts; that steps should be taken promptly to move in this direction; and that the first indispensable step is to remove the present inequity in the pay of men serving their first term in the armed forces.

The United States has relied throughout its history on a voluntary armed force except during major wars and since 1948. A return to an all-volunteer force will strengthen our freedoms, remove an inequity now imposed on the expression of the patriotism that has never been lacking among our youth, promote the efficiency of the armed forces, and enhance their dignity. It is the system for maintaining standing forces that minimizes government interference with the freedom of the individual to determine his own life in accord with his values.

The Commission bases its judgments on long-range considerations of what method of recruiting manpower will strengthen our society's foundations. The Commission's members have reached agreement on their recommendations only as the result of prolonged study and searching debate, and in spite of initial division. We are, of course, fully aware of the current and frequently emotional public debate on national priorities, foreign policy, and the military, but are agreed that such issues stand apart from the question of when and how to end conscription.

To judge the feasibility of an all-volunteer force, it is important to grasp the dimensions of the recruitment problem in the next decade. If conscription is continued, a stable mid-range force of 2.5 million men (slightly smaller than pre-Vietnam) will require 440,000 new enlisted men per year. To maintain a fully voluntary stable force of the same effective strength, taking into account lower personnel turnover, we estimate that not more than 325,000 men will have to be enlisted annually. In recent years about 500,000 men a year have volunteered for military service. Although some of these volunteered only because of the threat of the draft, the best estimates are that at least half—250,000 men—are "true volunteers." Such men would have volunteered even if there had been no draft, and they did volunteer in spite of an entry pay that is roughly 60 percent of the amount that men of their age, education, and training could earn in civilian life.

The often ignored fact, therefore, is that our present armed forces are made up predominantly of volunteers. All those men who have more than four years of service —38 percent of the total—are true volunteers; and so are at least a third of those with fewer than four years of service.

The return to voluntary means of raising and maintaining our armed forces should be seen in this perspective.

With true volunteers now providing some 250,000 enlisted men annually, a fully volunteer force of 2.5 million
men can be achieved by improving pay and conditions
of service sufficiently to induce approximately 75,000 additional young men to enlist each year from the 1.5 million
men who will annually turn 19 and who will also meet
the physical, moral, and mental requirements. A voluntary
force of 3.0 million men would require 400,000 enlistments each year, or 150,000 additional volunteers from
the 1.5 million eligible 19-year-olds. Smaller forces would
require fewer than 75,000 additional volunteers annually.
Reasonable improvements in pay and benefits in the early
years of service should increase the number of volunteers
by these amounts.

In any event, such improvements are called for on the
ground of equity alone. Because conscription has been
used to provide raw recruits, the pay of men entering
the services has been kept at a very low level. It has not
risen nearly as rapidly as the pay of experienced military
personnel, and it is now about 60 percent of comparable
civilian pay. Similarly, the pay of first-term officers has
not been kept in line with the pay of more experienced
officers, or with comparable civilians.

Correcting this inequity for first-term enlisted men and
first-term officers will add about $2.7 billion to the defense
budget in fiscal 1971. Regardless of the fate of the draft,
the Commission strongly recommends elimination of this
discrimination against first-termers.

If the Commission's recommendations are put into effect for fiscal 1971, they will entail a budget increase of
an estimated $3.3 billion for the following expenditures:

Basic pay increase	(Billions)	$2.68
Proficiency pay		.21
Reserve pay increase		.15
Additional medical corps expense		.12
Recruiting, ROTC, and miscellaneous		.08
		$3.24

The additional proficiency pay is required to attract
individuals in the first term with special skills and talents.
The additional reserve pay extends the increase in pay
provided for the active-duty forces to the reserves, and is

called for as a step toward a voluntary reserve. The additional outlay for a voluntary medical corps is for increased pay to medical officers, for medical student fellowships, and, where possible, for contracting with civilian physicians to provide medical services now rendered by military physicians.

Because most of this budget increase takes the form of personal income, $540 million of it will be recovered by the Treasury in federal income tax collections. The net increase in the budget in fiscal 1971, after taking these tax collections into account, will be $2.7 billion.

The Commission recommends that these additional funds be provided effective July 1, 1970. We believe, on the basis of our study, that the increased pay and other recommended improvements in personnel management will provide enough additional volunteers during the transition to achieve an all-volunteer force by July 1, 1971.

When force levels are stabilized, the additional expenditures needed in the transition to a voluntary force will be partly offset by savings engendered through lower turnover and a reduction in the number of persons in training status.

Combining the expenditures to eliminate the present inequity for first-termers, and other steps necessary to move to an all-volunteer force with the savings that will accrue, the Commission estimates that the added budget required to maintain a fully voluntary force on a stable, continuing basis is:

$1.5 billion for a 2,000,000-man force
$2.1 billion for a 2,500,000-man force
$4.6 billion for a 3,000,000-man force

These are net amounts, reflecting the personal income tax collections that would be recovered.

Although the *budgetary expense* of a volunteer armed force will be higher than for the present mixed force of volunteers and conscripts, the *actual cost* will be lower. This seemingly paradoxical statement is true because many of the costs of manning our armed forces today are hidden and are not reflected in the budget. Men who are forced to serve in the military at artificially low pay are actually paying a form of tax which subsidizes those in the society who do not serve. Furthermore, the output of the civilian economy is reduced because more men serve in the military than would be required for an all-volunteer force of the same strength. This cost does not show up in the budget. Neither does the loss in output resulting from the disruption in the lives of young men who do not serve. Neither do the costs borne by those men who do not serve, but who rearrange their lives in response to the possibility of being drafted. Taking these hidden and neglected costs into account, the actual cost to the nation of an all-volunteer force will be lower than the cost of the present force.

The Commission has attempted to allow for the uncertainties of the future. In the event of a national emergency requiring a rapid increase in the number of men under arms, the first recourse should be to ready reserves, including the National Guard. Like the active duty forces, these reserves can and should be recruited on a voluntary basis. Whatever advantages may be claimed for it, conscription cannot provide emergency forces: it takes many months of training for civilians to become soldiers. However, to provide for the possibility of an emergency requiring a major increase in forces over an extended period, we recommend that machinery be created for a standby draft, to take effect by act of Congress upon the recommendation of the President.

The draft has been an accepted feature of American life for a generation, and its elimination will represent still another major change in a society much buffeted by change and alarmed by violent attacks on the established order. Yet the status quo can be changed constructively and the society improved peacefully, by responsible and responsive government. It is in this spirit that the Commission has deliberated and arrived at its recommendations. However necessary conscription may have been in World War II, it has revealed many disadvantages in the past generation. It has been a costly, inequitable, and divisive procedure for recruiting men for the armed forces. It has imposed heavy burdens on a small minority of young men while easing slightly the tax burden on the rest of us. It has introduced needless uncertainty into the lives of all our young men. It has burdened draft boards with painful decisions about who shall be compelled to serve and who shall be deferred. It has weakened the political fabric of our society and impaired the delicate web of shared values that alone enables a free society to exist.

These costs of conscription would have to be borne if they were a necessary price for defending our peace and security. They are intolerable when there is an alternative consistent with our basic national values.

The alternative is an all-volunteer force, and the Commission recommends these steps toward it:

1. Raise the average level of basic pay for military personnel in the first two years of service from $180 a month to $315 a month, the increase to become effective on July 1, 1970. This involves an increase in total compensation (including the value of food, lodging, clothing, and fringe benefits) from $301 a month to $437 a month. The basic pay of officers in the first two years should be raised from an average level of $428 a month to $578 a month, and their total compensation from $717 a month to $869 a month.
2. Make comprehensive improvements in conditions of military service and in recruiting as set forth elsewhere in the report.
3. Establish a standby draft system by June 30, 1971, to be activated by joint resolution of Congress upon request of the President.

CHAPTER 2

The Debate

"We have lived with the draft so long," President Nixon
has pointed out, "that too many of us accept it as normal
and necessary." Over the past generation, social, political,
and economic arrangements have grown up around conscription that touch our lives in a great many ways. The
elimination of the draft will inevitably disrupt these
arrangements and may be disturbing to some. But beyond
these narrow, often overlooked interests lie broader considerations which have prompted defenders of conscription to argue that an all-volunteer armed force will have
a variety of undesirable political, social, and military
effects.

In our meetings we have discussed the opposing arguments extensively. As our recommendations disclose, we
have unanimously concluded that the arguments for an
all-volunteer force are much the stronger. Yet, there can
be no question of the sincerity and earnest conviction
of those who hold the views we have rejected. In fairness
to them, and to acquaint the nation with both sides of
the issues, this chapter summarizes the main arguments
raised against the volunteer force and offers answers to
them. In succeeding chapters (noted in parentheses) these
arguments are taken up in detail.

A general point should be made here. The elimination
of conscription admittedly is a major social change, but
it will not produce a major change in the personnel of our
armed forces. The majority of men serving today are
volunteers. And many who are now conscripted would
volunteer once improvements were made in pay and other

conditions of service. Therefore, the difference between an all-volunteer force and a mixed force of conscripts and volunteers is limited to that minority who would not serve unless conscripted and who would not volunteer in the absence of conscription. An all-volunteer force will attract men who are not now conscripted and who do not now volunteer but who will do so when military service imposes less of a financial penalty than it currently does.

Contrary to much dramatic argument, the reality is that an all-volunteer force will be manned largely by the same kind of individuals as today's armed forces. The men who serve will be quite similar in patriotism, political attitudes, effectiveness, and susceptibility to civilian control. The draft does not guarantee the quality of our armed forces, and neither will voluntarism. There are no simple solutions or shortcuts in dealing with the complex problems that must always concern us as a free people.

Arguments against an all-volunteer force fall into fairly distinct, though sometimes overlapping, categories, one of which is feasibility. Summarized below are some of the main objections under this heading.

Objection 1: An all-volunteer force will be very costly —so costly the nation cannot afford it.

Answer: The question of how much the armed forces cost is confused with the question of who bears those costs. It is true that the budget for a voluntary force will generally be higher than for an equally effective force of conscripts and volunteers; but the cost of the voluntary force will be less than the cost of the mixed force. This apparent paradox arises because some of the costs of a mixed force are hidden and never appear in the budget.

Under the present system, first-term servicemen must bear a disproportionately large share of the defense burden. Draftees and draft-induced volunteers are paid less than they would require to enlist without a draft. The loss they suffer is a tax-in-kind, which for budget purposes is never recorded as a receipt or an expenditure. We estimate that for draftees and draft-induced volunteers the total tax amounts to $2 billion per year; an average of $3,600 per man. If government accounts reflected as income this financial penalty imposed on first-term servicemen, it would become clear that a voluntary force costs less than a mixed force. One example of real cost savings that will accrue is the reduction in training costs as a result of the lower personnel turnover of a voluntary force.

Conscription also imposes social and human costs by distorting the personal life and career plans of the young and by forcing society to deal with such difficult problems as conscientious objection (chapter 3).

Objection 2: The all-volunteer force will lack the flexibility to expand rapidly in times of sudden crises.

Answer: Military preparedness depends on forces in being, not on the ability to draft untrained men. Reserve forces provide immediate support to active forces, while the draft provides only inexperienced civilians who must be organized, trained, and equipped before they can become effective soldiers and sailors—a process which takes many months. The Commission has recommended a standby draft which can be put into effect promptly if circumstances require mobilization of large numbers of men. History shows that Congress has quickly granted the authority to draft when needed (chapter 10).

Others contend that an all-volunteer force will have undesirable political and social effects. Some of these objections are given below.

Objection 3: An all-volunteer force will undermine patriotism by weakening the traditional belief that each citizen has a moral responsibility to serve his country.

Answer: Compelling service through a draft undermines respect for government by forcing an individual to serve when and in the manner the government decides, regardless of his own values and talents. Clearly, not all persons are equally suited for military service— some are simply not qualified. When not all our citizens can serve, and only a small minority are needed, a voluntary decision to serve is the best answer, morally and practically, to the question of who should serve (chapters 3 and 12).

Objection 4: The presence of draftees in a mixed force guards against the growth of a separate military ethos, which could pose a threat to civilian authority, our freedom, and our democratic institutions.

Answer: Historically voluntary service and freedom have gone hand in hand. In the United States and England, where voluntarism has been used most consistently, there is also the strongest tradition of civilian control of the military. There are responsibilities to be met in maintaining civilian control, but they must be exercised from above rather than at the lowest level of the enlisted ranks. They reside in the Halls of Congress, and in the White House as well as in the military hierarchy.

In either a mixed or volunteer force, the attitudes of the officer corps are the preponderant factor in the psychology of the military; and with or without the draft, professional officers are recruited voluntarily from a variety of regional and socioeconomic backgrounds. It is hard to believe that substituting a true volunteer for a draftee or a draft-induced volunteer in one of every six positions will so alter the military as to threaten the tradition of civilian control, which is embodied in the Constitution and deeply felt by the public. It is even less credible when one considers that this substitution will occur at the lowest level of the military ladder, among first-term enlisted men and officers, and that turnover of these first-term personnel in an all-volunteer force will be approximately three-fourths of that in a comparable mixed force.

The truth is, we already have a large professional armed force amounting to over 2 million men. The existing loyalties and political influence of that force cannot be materially changed by eliminating conscription in the lowest ranks (chapter 12).

Objection 5: The higher pay required for a voluntary force will be especially appealing to blacks, who have relatively poorer civilian opportunities. This, combined with higher re-enlistment rates for blacks, will mean that a disproportionate number of blacks will be in military service. White enlistments and re-enlistments might decline, thus leading to an all-black enlisted force. Racial tensions would grow because of white apprehension at this development and black resentment at bearing an undue share of the burden of defense. At the same time, some of the most qualified young blacks would be in the military—not in the community where their talents are needed.

Answer: The frequently heard claim that a volunteer force will be all black or all this or all that simply has no basis in fact. Our research indicates that the composition of the armed forces will not be fundamentally changed by ending conscription. Negroes presently make up 10.5 percent of the enlisted forces, slightly less than the proportion of blacks in the nation. Our best projections for the future are that blacks will be about 14 percent of the enlisted men in a conscripted force totaling 2.5 million officers and men, and 15 percent in an all-volunteer force of equal capability. For the Army, we estimate that the proportion of blacks will be 17 percent for the mixed force and 19 percent for the voluntary force as compared to 12.8 percent in the Army today. To be sure, these are estimates, but even extreme assumptions would not change the figures drastically.

If higher pay does make opportunities in an all-volunteer force more attractive to some particular group than those in civilian life, then the appropriate course is to correct the discriminations in civilian life —*not* to introduce additional discriminations against such a group.

The argument that blacks would bear an unfair share of the burden of an all-volunteer force confounds service by free choice with compulsory service. With conscription, some blacks are compelled to serve at earnings below what they would earn in the civilian economy. Blacks who join a voluntary force presumably have decided for themselves that military service is preferable to the other alternatives available to them. They regard military service as a more rewarding opportunity, not as a burden. Denial of this opportunity would reflect either bias or a paternalistic belief that blacks are not capable of making the "right" decisions concerning their lives (chapter 12).

Objection 6: Those joining an all-volunteer force will be men from the lowest economic classes, motivated primarily by monetary rewards rather than patriotism. An all-volunteer force will be manned, in effect, by mercenaries.

Answer: Again, our research indicates that an all-volunteer force will not differ significantly from the current force of conscripts and volunteers. Maintenance of current mental, physical, and moral standards for enlistment will ensure that a better paid, volunteer force will not recruit an undue proportion of youths from disadvantaged socioeconomic backgrounds. A disproportionate fraction of the 30 percent presently unable to meet these standards come from such backgrounds, and these men would also be ineligible for service in an all-volunteer force. Increasing military pay in the first term of service will increase the attractiveness of military service more to those who have higher civilian earnings potential than to those who have lower civilian potential. Military pay is already relatively attractive to those who have very poor civilian alternatives. If eligible, such individuals are now free to enlist and, moreover, are free to remain beyond their first term of service when military pay is even more attractive.

Finally, how will "mercenaries" suddenly emerge in the armed forces as a result of better pay and other conditions of service? The term "mercenary" applies to men who enlist for pay alone, usually in the service of a foreign power, and precludes all other motives for serving. Those who volunteer to serve in the armed forces do so for a variety of reasons, including a sense of duty. Eliminating the financial penalty first-term servicemen presently suffer, and improving other conditions of service, will not suddenly change the motives and basic attitudes of new recruits. Also, can we regard as mercenaries the career commissioned and noncommissioned officers now serving beyond their first term? (chapter 12).

Objection 7: An all-volunteer force would stimulate foreign military adventures, foster an irresponsible foreign policy, and lessen civilian concern about the use of military forces.

Answer: Decisions by a government to use force or to threaten the use of force during crises are extremely difficult. The high cost of military resources, the moral burden of risking human lives, political costs at home and overseas, and the overshadowing risk of nuclear confrontation—these and other factors enter into such decisions. It is absurd to argue that issues of such importance would be ignored and the decision for war made on the basis of whether our forces were entirely voluntary or mixed.

To the extent that there is pressure to seek military solutions to foreign policy problems, such pressure already exists and will not be affected by ending conscription. The volunteer force will have the same professional leadership as the present mixed force. Changes in the lower ranks will not alter the character of this leadership or the degree of civilian control.

A decision to use the all-volunteer force will be made according to the same criteria as the decision to use a mixed force of conscripts and volunteers because the size and readiness of the two forces will be quite similar. These military factors are key determinants in any decision to commit forces. Beyond initial commitment, the policy choice between expanding our forces by conscription or by voluntary enlistment is the same for both the all-volunteer force and a mixed force of conscripts and volunteers. The important difference between the two forces lies in the necessity for political debate before returning to conscription. With the all-volunteer force, the President can seek authorization to activate the standby draft, but Congress must give its consent. With the mixed system, draft calls can be increased by the President. The difference between the two alternatives is crucial. The former will generate public discussion of the use of the draft to fight a war; the latter can be done without such public discussion. If the need for conscription is not clear, such discussion will clarify the issue, and the draft will be used only if public support is widespread (chapter 12).

Other critics of an all-volunteer force argue that it will gradually erode the military's effectiveness. Some of their main concerns are taken up below.

Objection 8: A voluntary force will be less effective because not enough highly qualified youths will be likely to enlist and pursue military careers. As the quality of servicemen declines, the prestige and dignity of the services will also decline and further intensify recruiting problems.

Answer: The Commission has been impressed by the number and quality of the individuals who, despite conscription, now choose a career in the military. The fact that we must resort in part to coercion to man the armed services must be a serious deterrent to potential volunteers. A force made up of men freely choosing to serve should enhance the dignity and prestige of the military. Every man in uniform will be serving as a matter of choice rather than coercion.

The Commission recognizes the importance of recruiting and retaining qualified individuals. It has recommended improved basic compensation and conditions of service, proficiency pay, and accelerated promotions for the highly skilled to make military career opportunities more attractive. These improvements, combined with an intensive recruiting effort, should enable the military not only to maintain a high quality force but also to have one that is more experienced, better motivated, and has higher morale (chapters 4, 5, 7, and 12).

Objection 9: The defense budget will not be increased to provide for an all-volunteer force, and the Department of Defense will have to cut back expenditures in other areas. Even if additional funds are provided initially, competing demands will, over the long term, force the Department of Defense to absorb the added budgetary expense of an all-volunteer force. The result could be a potentially serious deterioration of the nation's overall military posture.

Answer: Ultimately, the size of the military budget and the strength of our armed forces depend upon public attitudes toward national defense. Since World War II, our peacetime armed forces have been consistently supported at high levels. The public has supported large forces because it has felt them essential to national security. The change from a mixed force of volunteers and conscripts to an all-volunteer force cannot significantly change that feeling.

The contention that an all-volunteer force is undesirable because it would result in smaller defense forces raises a serious issue regarding the conduct of government in a democracy. Conscription obscures a part of the cost of providing manpower for defense. When that cost is made explicit, taxpayers may decide they prefer a smaller defense force. If so, the issue has been resolved openly, in accord with the Constitution, and in the best tradition of the democratic process. Those who then argue that too little is being devoted to national defense are saying that they are unwilling to trust the open democratic process; that, if necessary, a hidden tax should be imposed to support the forces they believe are necessary (chapters 3 and 12).

PART II

CHAPTER 3

Conscription Is a Tax

Any government has essentially two ways of accomplishing an objective whether it be building an interstate highway system or raising an army. It can expropriate the required tools and compel construction men and others to work until the job is finished or it can purchase the goods and manpower necessary to complete the job. Under the first alternative, only the persons who own the property seized or who render compulsory services are required to bear the expense of building the highway or housing project. They pay a tax to finance the project, albeit a tax-in-kind. Under the second alternative, the cost of the necessary goods and services is borne by the general public through taxes raised to finance the project.

Conscription is like the first alternative—a tax-in-kind. A mixed force of volunteers and conscripts contains first-term servicemen of three types—(1) draftees, (2) draft-induced volunteers, and (3) true volunteers. Draftees and draft-induced volunteers in such a force are coerced into serving at levels of compensation below what would be required to induce them to volunteer. They are, in short, underpaid. This underpayment is a form of taxation. Over 200 years ago, Benjamin Franklin, in commenting on a judicial opinion concerning the legality of impressment of American merchant seamen, recognized the heart of the issue, and even estimated the hidden tax. He wrote:

"But if, as I suppose is often the case, the sailor who is pressed and obliged to serve for the defence of this trade at the rate of 25s. a month, could have £3.15s, in the merchant's service, you take from him 50s. a month; and if you have

100,000 in your service, you rob that honest part of society and their poor families of £250,000. per month, or three millions a year, and at the same time oblige them to hazard their lives in fighting for the defence of your trade; to the defence of which all ought indeed to contribute, (and sailors among the rest) in proportion to their profits by it; but this three millions is more than their share, if they did not pay with their persons; and when you force that, methinks you should excuse the other.

"But it may be said, to give the king's seamen merchant's wages would cost the nation too much, and call for more taxes. The question then will amount to this; whether it be just in a community, that the richer part should compel the poorer to fight for them and their properties for such wages as they think fit to allow, and punish them if they refuse? Our author tells us it is *legal*. I have not law enough to dispute his authority, but I cannot persuade myself it is *equitable*."

The levy of taxes-in-kind is not a modern innovation. Such taxes have existed throughout history. The impressment to which Benjamin Franklin objected is an example. Also, it was common practice in the Middle Ages to require specific service of citizens in farming, construction, defense, and other activities. Traditionally, however, in the United States, taxes-in-kind have been rejected for three reasons. First, they deprive individuals of their freedom to pursue their careers where and how they choose— in essence their right to liberty and the pursuit of happiness. Second, they are often accompanied by serious inequities; i.e., a few people are forced to bear the burden of accomplishing a task for the general good of the government and its citizens. Third, they tend to conceal taxes and government expenditures so that both the general public and public officials are misinformed as to the costs of government services.

Under conscription, each inductee and reluctant volunteer is compelled to render services to the government. He is required to pay a tax—a tax paid (and collected) in kind rather than cash—but the form of the payment does not alter the substance of the relationship. The amount of the tax is the difference between the pay that the inductee or reluctant volunteer actually receives as a first-term serviceman and the pay that would be required to induce him to enlist. Even true volunteers who serve in a mixed force are paid less than they would receive in a volunteer force. In that sense, they too are taxed by conscription.

Prevailing government accounting practices do not recognize taxes paid in kind. Therefore, the tax on first-term servicemen never gets recorded in the budget either as revenue or as expenditure. In an all-volunteer force, the additional military compensation will be paid in cash or other benefits, and the taxes to make those payments will be collected in cash. Recorded budget expenditures will have to be increased to reflect these payments. This is the source of the budget "increase" we have estimated for an all-volunteer force. If current government accounting practices fully reflected revenues and expenditures, whether in money or in kind, there would be *not* a budget increase, but a budget decrease.

The real significance of the larger recorded budget for an all-volunteer force is the adjustment of the burden of defense costs. What appears on the surface to be an increase in expenditures is actually a shift in the tax burden from first-term servicemen to taxpayers at large. If government accounts reflected taxes-in-kind, tax revenues from first-term servicemen would go down with the inauguration of an all-volunteer armed force, and (assuming a balanced budget) tax revenues from the general public would go up.

This shift in tax burden lies at the heart of resistance on "cost" grounds to an all-volunteer armed force. Indeed, this shift in tax burden explains how conscription gets enacted in the first place. In a political democracy conscription offers the general public an opportunity to impose a disproportionate share of defense costs on a minority of the population.

We have made estimates of the amount of the tax-in-kind imposed on draftees and draft-induced enlistees for the period immediately prior to Vietnam, adjusted to reflect changes in civilian and military compensation through 1969. The tax can be separated into two components: first, the financial loss suffered by draftees and draft-induced enlistees because their total military compensation (including veterans benefits) falls short of the income they would have earned in civilian life; and second, the additional burden measured by the excess of military over civilian compensation that would be required to induce these same individuals to become true volunteers. We estimate that the financial loss due to the first of these, the difference between military compensation and potential civilian earnings, was $1.5 billion for draftees or draft-induced volunteers in the pre-Vietnam force. To induce these same individuals to become true volunteers we estimate would have required an additional $500 million. Thus the total implicit tax on draftees and draft-induced volunteers was $2.0 billion.

This implies an average tax rate of 48 percent of the income that draftees and draft-induced enlistees would have earned in civilian life. Taking into account the personal income tax they paid, their total tax rate was 51 percent. In 1967, the average personal income tax paid by all persons whose gross earnings were equal to the amount that would have been earned by draftees and draft-induced enlistees as civilians was less than 10 percent of that gross income. Since draftees and draft-induced enlistees have fewer than the average number of dependents, it is estimated that they would have paid perhaps as much as 15 percent of their gross income in personal income tax. Hence, draftees and draft-induced enlistees are bearing a tax burden over three times that of comparable civilians.

This concept of the tax does not include the income loss suffered by true volunteers whose military compensation is held below the level which would be required to maintain an all-volunteer force, nor does it include the amount by which all-volunteer pay rates would exceed the pay levels at which some of the current draftees and draft-induced enlistees would enter on a voluntary basis. The sum of these two amounts has been estimated at $1.25 billion annually, again for the period immediately prior to Vietnam.

As is pointed out in detail later in this chapter, the concept of the implicit tax considered above does not fully encompass the costs of conscription. Prospective inductees also incur costs in their efforts to escape conscription—costs which manifest themselves in a variety of ways such as additional college attendance, movement into occupations which carry deferments, emigration, etc. Indirect evidence suggests that these costs may be 1.5 times the implicit tax, or about $3.0 billion. They can be viewed as the cost of collecting the implicit tax. Thus for each $1.00 of tax-in-kind collected, an average of $2.50 is forgone by the public. Quite apart from considerations of equity and freedom, this feature of conscription is enough to call it into question.

The fact that conscription imposes a tax is not in itself immoral and undesirable. Taxes are required to enable government to exist. What is of questionable morality is the discriminatory form that this implicit tax takes; and even more, the abridgement of individual freedom that is involved in collecting it.

The tax is discriminatory because the first-term servicemen who pay it constitute a small proportion of the total population. During the next decade the number of males reaching age 19 each year will average 2.2 million. To maintain a stable mixed force of 2.5 million men at present relative military/civilian pay levels, draft calls will average about 100,000 per year. We estimate that draft-induced enlistments might be 75,000 per year. Therefore the draftees and draft-induced enlistees paying the tax-in-kind will represent only 8 percent of the male population reaching age 19 each year.

The extent of the discrimination resulting from conscription depends on the proportion of the population forced to serve, and on the level of compensation provided to those' who serve. When a large fraction of the population is conscripted as it was, for example, in World War II, the tax is levied on a larger fraction of the population. Even then, however, the discrimination is by no means eliminated. Not everyone eligible to serve does so. Moreover, such wars do not occur every generation, hence some generations never pay though they benefit from the defense provided by others. Even in World War II, the 16.4 million men who served in the armed forces represented only 12 percent of the total population, 17 percent of the adult population, and 56 percent of the adult male population between 18 and 45.

Defenders of conscription often argue that every young person has the duty to serve his country. The above discussion makes it clear that the real question is not whether young people have such a duty, but whether that duty does not extend to the entire populace. Is it right and proper that a large tax be confined to a small fraction of our young able-bodied males in order to relieve taxpayers in general from having to pay higher taxes?

In addition to being discriminatory, conscription as a tax is also generally regressive, falling on individuals whose income is low. The amount of benefits in the form of defense that individuals receive as a consequence of the tax is not related to the amount of tax they pay. Finally, and most importantly, the tax requires payment in kind, rather than money, and the payment in kind takes the form of involuntary service.

It is unlikely that any Congressman would ever propose enactment of a general tax of the kind now imposed by the draft. If one ever were proposed, it would have little chance of being approved by Congress. If approved by Congress, it is hard to imagine that it would be held constitutional by the courts. This is a hidden tax which persists only because it is obscure. No tax is perfect, of course, but it is hard to imagine a means of imposing the cost of defense, or any other government activity for that matter, more in conflict with accepted standards of justice, equality, and freedom in the United States.

The Cost of an All-Volunteer Force

The larger budget required to sustain an all-volunteer armed force is frequently referred to as the "cost" of such a force. We have deliberately refrained from using that language. We have done so in order to stress the difference between "costs" on the one hand and "budget expenditures" on the other. Budget expenditures need not correctly reflect costs. Indeed, as we have indicated above, government accounting practices do not recognize the expenditure-in-kind implicit in conscription. To that extent the cost of a mixed voluntary/conscript force is consistently understated in the budget. But the cost of such a force is also understated in other ways.

When the hidden costs of conscription are fully recognized, the cost of an all-volunteer armed force is unquestionably less than the cost of a force of equal size and quality manned wholly or partly through conscription. The all-volunteer costs are lower for four reasons.

1. Conscription leads to low re-enlistment rates among first-term servicemen, thereby increasing turnover rates. Most inductees and draft-induced volunteers are not seriously interested in careers in the military. First-term re-enlistment rates for inductees pre-Vietnam were about one-fourth as high as for enlistees. In an all-volunteer force, first-term re-enlistment rates will be higher than those currently experienced because those who enlist will be more likely to choose the military as a career. Moreover, the term of service for inductees is only two years while regular Army enlistments are three years and Air Force and Navy enlistments are four years. With an all-volunteer force these longer terms of enlistment will also reduce turnover and the need for accessions.

Both factors will generate real savings. For a mixed voluntary/conscript force of 2.5 million men we estimate that annual first-term accessions in FY (fiscal year) 1977 to 1979 would have to be 452,000. For an all-volunteer force with equal effectiveness, accessions would be only 342,000, or 110,000 less. Lower accessions will mean a smaller training establishment; that is, fewer trainers, trainees, and support personnel and less training equipment and facilities. We estimate this will reduce the cost of a stable 2.5 million man peacetime force by $675 million per year.

In addition to the savings in training costs, there will also be savings in the number of personnel who are in a non-effective status because of transfers generated by high personnel turnover. An all-volunteer force will have fewer separations, hence fewer changes of status to accommodate separations. This also will result in cost savings. The number of servicemen in non-effective status will decline as will transportation and administrative costs. We estimate that these savings will be $68 million per year for a stable peacetime force of 2.5 million men.

In our study we have recognized these particular cost

reductions by appropriately reducing the required size of the forces. Thus, a mixed voluntary/conscript force of 2.5 million men is equated to an all-volunteer force of 2.44 million. The latter represents the same effective force as the former taking account of the savings in training and transients which we estimate will accrue.

2. Conscription induces the military services to use manpower inefficiently. They make manpower decisions on the basis of the costs as they perceive them, namely, those that are reflected in their budget. Because budget expenses significantly understate the cost of first-term servicemen, the services are led to use more of them than they otherwise would. This is not because they are profligate or inept. By minimizing the costs as they see them of meeting specific security requirements, they are behaving as the nation would want them to behave. The problem arises because conscription greatly understates these costs.

When military compensation is raised to a level consistent with an all-volunteer armed force, the services will find it desirable to economize on manpower. In particular, they will discover ways to substitute non-human resources for manpower in a wide variety of activities. They will find it desirable to mechanize tasks now performed manually, and to emphasize, even more than at present, durability, reliability, and ease of maintenance in the design of equipment and vehicles and in the construction of facilities. It would be a prodigious research effort to examine each activity for potential savings from such substitutions. Moreover, as a practical matter, there will be a long period of transition before the process of effecting such substitutions is completed. For these reasons we have not attempted to estimate the total savings that could result from labor-saving substitutions if the forces were all-volunteer.

We have, however, examined one area of potential substitutions; namely, that of using civilians instead of military personnel in particular positions. Conscription leads to the assignment of servicemen to some billets which could be filled by civilians at lower costs. If a civilian is hired, the Defense Department must pay the full cost thereof, but if a first-term serviceman is used the price is only his military compensation. An extensive study was conducted of specific billets where potential savings from such substitutions exist. These savings accrue because military training costs are reduced or because a civilian can be hired at a salary below the real cost of a service-man performing the same task, that is, below the salary required to fill the position with a volunteer. We estimate that for a force of 2.5 million men, 117,000 civilians could be substituted for servicemen at a savings of per-haps $100 million per year.

3. Conscription, whether by lottery or on a selective basis, is relatively insensitive to the alternative value of the draftee in the civilian economy and to his tastes for military employment. Thus, suppose a draftee or draft-induced volunteer is compelled to enter the service who would do so voluntarily only if he were offered $8,000 per year. If there exists a true volunteer who would be equally productive in the military, prepared to enlist for $6,000 per year, the difference of $2,000 is an additional real cost imposed by the draft. The $2,000 can reflect either a difference in the productivity of the two persons in the civilian economy, or differences in taste for military life. Whichever it is, the loss is a real cost (and a waste) in precisely the same sense as is any other cost.

4. Finally, there are many subtle costs imposed by con-scription that are no less real for their subtlety. Their effects ramify throughout society, impinging on a variety of individual and institutional decisions.

The costs imposed on potential draftees are perhaps the most obvious. The draft erodes ideals of patriotism and service by alienating many of the young who bear its burden. American youths are raised in an atmosphere where freedom and justice are held dear. It is difficult for them to cope with a situation which falls far short of these ideals just as they enter adulthood. The draft under-mines identification with society just at the age when young men begin to assume social responsibilities. It thwarts the natural desire of youths to commit them-selves to society.

Many of the implicit costs of the draft arise out of the

system of deferments and exemptions currently in effect, and out of the qualification requirements for military service. Young men distort their career and personal plans to take advantage of opportunities to postpone or avoid being drafted. They enter college when they otherwise would not. They stay in school longer than they otherwise would. They accept employment in positions they otherwise would not take. They marry and have families before they otherwise would. There is no doubt that the costs of these distorted choices are real and often cruelly high. Popular support for making 19 the year of primary draft eligibility stems largely from the desire to reduce uncertainty and improve opportunity for personal planning. "Channeling" young men into colleges, occupations, marriage, or fatherhood is not in their best interests nor those of society as a whole.

The procedures of the Selective Service System also impose hidden costs. In many ways the young registrant is denied due process of law. He is confronted with an intricate legal maze and denied the right of counsel and judicial review during its normal operation. To get his case before the courts, the potential draftee must risk jail sentences of up to five years. The operation of the draft abridges constitutional rights in many other ways. For example, a registrant must get permission to travel outside the country. In addition to the loss of rights, there is the problem of determining who is entitled to exemption as a conscientious objector. These decisions are inherently difficult to make, and are harmful both to the group deciding and the persons requesting conscientious objector status. The process weakens the political fabric of our society and threatens the delicate web of shared values that alone enables a free society to exist. These problems are completely avoided by an all-volunteer force.

Each problem faced by the individual registrant has a counterpart in the institutions with which he must deal. In addition to draft-induced volunteers for the military, selective service results in draft-induced college students, draft-induced ministerial students, draft-induced husbands and fathers, and draft-induced employees in exempt occupations.

The draft creates unnecessary problems for the military. Selection by lottery compels some to serve who have neither a talent nor a taste for military life, resulting in misfits and maladjustments to military service. Draftees who cannot adjust must nevertheless serve out a two-year tour. These men present morale and disciplinary problems which otherwise would not arise. Some spend much of their military service in confinement, because it is so difficult for them to adjust to military service. Dissent within the military presents particularly ticklish problems for the armed forces of a free nation. The problems raised by the forced military service of those who are unwilling or unable to adjust to military life will be largely overcome by voluntary recruiting.

Because of the influence of the draft, our schools and colleges must choose among more applicants than would normally apply. Inevitably they admit some young men more interested in exemptions than education. The presence of these individuals adds to the forces of disruption on the campus, imposing costs on all members of a university community.

Employers, too, must sort out true volunteers from draft-induced applicants for jobs which provide exemptions. For example, when school teachers are deferred, some young men will become teachers for a short time, even though they would rather follow another profession. They will stay in teaching only as long as they require an occupational deferment. This results in higher turnover and less experienced and less dedicated teachers for the young of the country.

It is difficult to add up these costs and measure their overall impact on society. Yet it is easy to cite examples of serious problems created by the draft, which voluntary recruiting would eliminate.

CHAPTER 4

Military Personnel Requirements

In planning for an all-volunteer armed force, the size and quality of future military forces are critical variables. Small forces or those of low quality could be raised on a voluntary basis, even if military compensation were reduced. Very large forces or those of high quality would require substantial increases in military pay.

The size of active duty forces since World War II, shown in table 4-I, has fluctuated widely. After reaching a peak of 3.6 million men during the Korean War, the armed forces slowly declined in size toward an apparent equilibrium level of 2.5 to 2.6 million men. Although the Vietnam War reversed this trend, the President's budget message of April 1969 suggested that, in a post-Vietnam environment, active duty force levels be stabilized at a level of 2.0 to 2.5 million men.

Because of the uncertainties surrounding force plans for a post-Vietnam environment, the Commission decided to analyze the manpower and budgetary implications of four alternative active duty force levels, 2.0, 2.25, 2.5, and 3.0 million men. These four force levels cover a reasonable range of alternative peacetime active duty forces that might be needed to insure national security.

The armed services' demand for the nation's manpower resources is indicated by the size of the active duty forces as a percentage of the male population 18–45 years of age, shown in the last column of table 4-I. The comparatively small force of 2.5 million men in FY 1960 represented 7.9 percent of this male population. In light of the projected growth of the male population, all four alternative

34

TABLE 4–I.—Active duty force strength
[selected fiscal years 1950–69 and projections]

Fiscal year	Total DOD (Dept. of Defense) (millions)	Active duty as percent of 18–45 male population
1950..........	1.46	4.8
1953..........	3.56	11.6
1955..........	2.94	9.6
1960..........	2.48	7.9
1965..........	2.66	8.0
1969..........	3.49	9.8
Alternative projected forces		
1975..........	3.00	7.4
	2.50	6.1
	2.25	5.5
	2.00	4.9

force levels constitute smaller percentages of the projected 18-to-45-year-old male population in 1975.

Over the past two decades, the structure of the armed forces has changed substantially (see table 4-II). The service structure is important because the Army is the only service that has consistently required draftees to meet its strength objectives. (The Navy and Marine Corps have occasionally issued draft calls to meet temporary shortfalls, but the Air Force has never used the draft.) Prior to Korea, the Army made up 41 percent of all active duty forces. The post-Korean reduction in forces of the late 1950's was accompanied by a shift which gave larger shares of the defense responsibility to the Navy and Air Force. Since the escalation of American involvement in Vietnam, the ground combat forces of the Army and Marine Corps have become a larger fraction of the force, as shown in table 4-II. The service distribution of the four future forces shown in table 4-II reflects a slight reversal of the trend of the late 1950's. The Army, for example, represents 40 percent of the 2.5-million-man force compared with only 35 percent for the 1960 active duty force. The relative size of the Army in force plans is important because the projected shortfalls in recruitment are largest for the Army.

TABLE 4–II.—

Distribution of active duty force strength by service
[selected fiscal years 1950–69 and projections]

Fiscal year	Distribution (percent)			
	Army	Navy	Marine Corps	Air Force
1950.........	41	26	5	28
1953.........	43	22	7	28
1955.........	38	22	7	33
1960.........	35	25	7	33
1965.........	37	25	7	31
1969.........	44	22	9	25
Alternative forces (millions)				
3.00.........	43	24	8	25
2.50.........	40	24	8	27
2.25.........	37	25	9	29
2.00.........	37	26	8	29

Substantial numbers of civilians and reservists supplement the active duty forces in the overall defense manpower picture, as shown in table 4-III. The ratio of civilians to active duty personnel [column (5) of table 4-III] has declined over the past 15 years. Many positions in the force structure currently manned by uniformed servicemen could be staffed with civilians at lower budgetary costs and with no loss in immediate effectiveness. In addition, the substitution of civilians for servicemen reduces the demands for new recruits. Civilians typically need less training, involve fewer transfers of personnel, and require lower levels of compensation, especially in an all-volunteer force. Civilians, however, are only imperfect substitutes for uniformed personnel, because they cannot be involuntarily mobilized and moved in the event of an emergency. The scope of civilian substitutions is further limited by the military's need to provide positions for rotational assignments and career development.

A position-by-position analysis of the opportunities for civilian substitution was not possible within the scope of

TABLE 4–III.—Active duty, civilian, and paid drill reserve strength [in thousands] FY 1947–1969

(1)	(2)	(3)	(4)	(5)	(6)
			Paid	Ratios:	Ratios:
Fiscal	Total	Total	drill	civ/	paid drill/
year	DOD *	civilian	reserve	DOD	DOD
1947....	1,583	1,060	231	.67	.15
1952....	3,636	1,650	506	.45	.14
1957....	2,796	1,429	1,047	.51	.37
1962....	2,808	1,241	889	.44	.32
1965....	2,655	1,164	933	.44	.35
1969....	3,460	1,456	960	.42	.28

* Active duty military personnel only.

this study because of limitations of time and resources. However, a careful aggregative study of individual occupational specialties was conducted, ranking the various occupations by the degree to which they were purely military. This study concludes that approximately 95,000 positions in a force of 2 million men could be staffed by civilians with no loss in effectiveness. Larger civilian substitutions could be achieved at larger force levels. The budgetary savings (in constant 1969 prices) which would result from carrying out the proposed civilian substitution programs range from $90 million for the 2-million-man force to $125 million for the 3-million-man force. If these programs are implemented, the proportion of total defense manpower which is civilian will increase from 31 percent to about 34 percent, thereby reversing the trend of the past 15 years.

The reductions in the size of each of the active duty uniformed forces that would result from civilian substitution are shown in table 4-IV. The impact of civilian substitution on required accessions is slow to take effect, and its full impact is not felt until 1978. Rotation policies and the size of overseas deployment have an important effect on the potential for civilian substitutions. The potential is greatest in the Air Force, where the majority of the force is stationed in the continental United States. In the Army and Marine Corps the opportunities are limited by relatively large overseas deployments and rotation policies.

TABLE 4–IV.—Substitution potential: all services
[in thousands]

Size force	Army	Navy	USMC	USAF	DOD
2.0 million					
Officer	5.2	5.1	0.6	9.4	20.3
Enlisted ..	0.0	8.8	6.8	59.7	75.3
Total ...	5.2	13.9	7.4	69.1	95.6
2.25 million					
Officer	5.9	5.6	0.7	10.3	22.5
Enlisted ..	0.0	9.8	7.9	66.0	83.7
Total ...	5.9	15.4	8.6	76.3	106.2
2.5 million					
Officer	6.6	6.2	0.8	11.3	24.9
Enlisted ..	0.0	10.8	8.9	72.2	91.9
Total ...	6.6	17.0	9.7	83.5	116.8
3.0 million					
Officer	8.9	7.0	0.9	12.4	29.2
Enlisted ..	0.0	12.1	10.2	79.1	101.4
Total ...	8.9	19.1	11.1	91.5	130.6

When the forces have reached their post-Vietnam equilibrium levels, a program of civilian substitutions should be initiated and carried out over a three-to-four-year period. Too rapid replacement of uniformed personnel by civilians might seriously impair the attractiveness of military careers. It is also recommended that civilian manpower ceilings be relaxed to enable the Department of Defense to follow more rational manpower management policies. Prior attempts to accomplish civilian substitution (in fiscal years 1952, 1955, 1962, and 1965) were curtailed, abandoned, or even reversed because of civilian manpower and budget ceilings. The Department of Defense ought to have the flexibility to vary the ratio of civilians to military personnel within a total budget constraint. To establish an economic balance between civilian and military personnel, the Department of Defense should undertake a position-by-position analysis, review the criteria to determine whether a particular position should be military or civilian, and develop better data to estimate the real economic costs of military and civilian personnel.

Trained reservists provided much of the manpower for the rapid expansions of active duty forces during the Korean War and the Berlin crisis of 1961-62. However, reserves have not been activated in significant numbers for the Vietnam War. Reference to table 4-III reveals that the size of the paid reserve forces has remained stable over the past decade. Details regarding the size and composition of the reserves in an all-volunteer force are more fully discussed in Chapter 9.

Effective Force Strengths

The size of the active duty forces does not directly reflect defense capability. The servicemen who have already completed basic military and technical training are the ones who provide defense capability. Recruits, instructors, and support personnel at training bases only indirectly contribute to defense by supplying future trained personnel. In addition to these non-effective training billets, other positions in the active force structure must be set aside for personnel in transit between duty assignments or interned as patients and prisoners. With lower personnel turnover, each recruit spends a smaller fraction of his service career in training or in other forms of non-effective status. Because it will have fewer non-effective men, an all-volunteer force can be smaller than a mixed force of conscripts and volunteers but still provide the same effective strength.

Personnel turnover in an all-volunteer force will be reduced for several reasons. If the draft is continued, it is projected that about 42 percent of accessions into the Army (for a force of 2.5 million men) will be draftees who serve for only two years, compared with three- and four-year tours for voluntary enlistments. Moreover, the re-enlistment rates of draftees and draft-motivated volunteers are considerably lower than those of men who voluntarily choose military service. Finally, the pay increase needed to move to an all-volunteer force includes somewhat higher pay for second-term enlisted men, which will further increase the re-enlistment rate.

When these factors are taken into account, we estimate that the turnover of enlisted personnel in an all-volunteer Army will be only 17 percent per year, compared with 26 percent for a mixed conscript/volunteer Army of the same size. With this reduction in turnover, the enlisted strength of an all-volunteer force could be 5 percent less than that of a mixed force, while retaining the same number of effective men in non-training and non-transient positions. Put another way, 13 percent of a mixed force is assigned to non-effective positions at training bases or in transit, while only 9 percent of the all-volunteer force will be so occupied. These manpower savings are greatest for the Army, which is projected to realize the sharpest reduction in personnel turnover rates as a result of moving to a voluntary system.

In developing estimates of overall accession requirements for uniformed personnel, the sizes of all volunteer forces were reduced to provide the same effective strengths as the four mixed forces in table 4-II. The manpower savings that derive from lower personnel turnover are evident from the data in table 4-V, which show enlisted strengths for forces of equal effectiveness.

TABLE 4–V.—Equal effectiveness all-volunteer and draft forces [in thousands]

Total strength (in millions)	DOD enlisted strength (draft)	DOD enlisted strength (all-volunteer)	Army enlisted strength (draft)	Army enlisted strength (all-volunteer)
2.0	1,713	1,683	642	624
2.25....	1,930	1,886	721	692
2.5	2,146	2,089	868	827
3.0	2,597	2,559	1,120	1,047

The higher retention rate for true volunteers inevitably produces a more experienced force. Our projections indicate that, by 1980, 45 percent of Army enlisted men will have four years or more of service experience, as compared with 31 percent for a mixed force of the same size.

Since experience involves on-the-job training, a more experienced force is more productive than a less experienced one. Military officers agree that one career enlisted man is worth more than one first-term serviceman, but few officers are willing to indicate the precise trade-offs. Although the all-volunteer and mixed forces in table 4-V have the same numbers of effective men in non-training and non-transient positions, the all-volunteer forces actually provide greater effectiveness because they possess more experience.

The concept of effective force strength is equally applicable to officers. Because officers typically receive their training before they are commissioned, it is difficult to estimate their non-effective training time. Moreover, training times and costs vary widely, being highest for an Academy graduate who goes on to flight training, and lowest for a chaplain who receives a direct appointment.

In estimating the budgetary savings resulting from lower turnover among commissioned officers, we have disregarded non-effective training times. We have instead based our estimates on the average cost of $12,000 for training an officer in either the college or non-college officer training schools that have been used in the past to meet fluctuating demands for officers.

Required Accessions Under Alternative Manpower Procurement Systems

The flow of accessions (voluntary enlistments and draftees) required to maintain a given force depends on the size of the force and the losses from active duty ranks. These requirements can be met either on a purely voluntary basis or through a mixture of enlistments and inductions. With an all-volunteer force, smaller flows are required for two reasons. First, true volunteers serve longer, thereby reducing losses due to separations upon completion of initial obligated tours. Second, the same effective force strength can be maintained with a smaller total active duty force.

The annual flows of accessions required to sustain the four mixed force levels using a lottery draft are presented in the first and third columns of table 4-VI. If the draft is abolished and all recruits are true volunteers, the same effective force strength can be maintained by the smaller annual flows of required accessions shown in the last two columns of table 4-VI. An all-volunteer force with the same effective strength as a 2.5-million-man mixed force requires 25 percent fewer accessions per year than the mixed force. The reduction in required accessions resulting from the move to an all-volunteer force is considerably

TABLE 4–VI.—Required accessions to enlisted ranks [annual averages FY 1979–81 in thousands]

| DOD total strength (in millions) | Continued draft | | | All-volunteer | |
	DOD	Army draft calls	Army	DOD	Army
2.0	312	19	138	259	104
2.25....	362	46	170	290	118
2.5	440	98	235	332	148
3.0	584	184	340	410	192

smaller for officers. The projections in table 4-VI pertain to the period 1979–81 after the greater retention rates for an all-volunteer force have taken effect. In the transition to stable force levels, accession requirements for the all-volunteer forces are slightly higher, especially in the case of the Army, where the average annual requirements for FY 1973–75 are 188 thousand, compared with 148 thousand for FY 1979–81.

Qualitative Characteristics of the Active Duty Forces

Members of the armed services today must possess more skills than their predecessors in World War II and Korea. This trend is indicated by the data in table 4-VII which shows the occupational mix of enlisted men in the Department of Defense and the Army. In 1953, 18 percent of all enlisted men were assigned to ground combat occupations that require comparatively little technical skill. The proportion of enlisted men in these relatively unskilled occupations has declined over time. Indeed, the projections of the force structure in a post-Vietnam environment show that only 10 percent will be in the ground combat forces. The declining importance of the ground combat forces cannot be attributed to a relative reduction in the size of the Army. In the Army occupational structure, the percentage of enlisted men in the ground combat occupations is projected to fall from 29 percent in FY 1963 to 21 percent in the forces of tomorrow. The services' demand for highly skilled men to staff electronics and other technical occupations has climbed over time.

TABLE 4–VII.—Percentage distribution of enlisted men by major occupation [selected fiscal years, 1945–74]

Occupation	1945	1953	1957	1963	1969*	1974*
Department of Defense:						
Ground combat ...	23	18	14	14	15	10
Electronics	6	10	13	15	10	11
Other technicians .	7	7	8	8	14	17
Adm/clerical	15	20	18	19	18	18
Mechanics	22	23	26	25	24	24
Craftsmen	11	7	8	7	7	7
Services	16	15	13	12	12	13
Army:						
Ground combat ...	39	35	32	29	26	21
Electronics	4	5	9	9	7	7
Other technicians ..	7	7	8	9	15	16
Adm/clerical	15	19	16	19	19	22
Mechanics	9	12	14	16	16	17
Craftsmen	7	3	5	4	4	4
Services	19	19	16	14	13	13

* The "Other Technicians" include the three major DOD occupations for Communications/Intelligence, Medical Corps, and Other Technical. The DOD figures are weighted averages based on enlisted force strengths. The percentages of DOD that were in the Army were respectively 50.4, 43.7, 36.2, 36.7, 44.4, and 39.0 for the 6 years shown in this table.

Source: H. Wool, *The Military Specialist*, p. 43, and special Service tabulations. (Copyrighted material.)

Two features of the changing occupational structure of the armed services are important. An increased demand for skilled personnel characterizes the civilian economy as well as the services. Thus, the services must compete with the civilian sector for those youths who in increasing numbers enter the labor force with more education and greater technical background than young men two decades ago. The other aspect of this phenomenon is the growing similarity of the military's skill requirements to those of the civilian sector. Various estimates suggest that 20 to 30 percent of active duty billets are directly related to combat missions. The remaining positions are required for logistical support, administration, maintenance, and training—all of which have counterparts in the civilian economy.

Qualification Standards for Enlisted Men

Admission to the enlisted ranks of the military services is now limited to men who satisfy three kinds of criteria: mental, physical, and moral. The physical and moral standards have remained stable over the past two decades. Although mental standards have exhibited some short-run variations, they have generally risen over time. The mental ability of a recruit is measured by his score on the Armed Forces Qualification Test (AFQT). Recruits are divided into five mental groups. Men in the lowest mental group, group V, are exempt by law from military service. The mental group distribution of accessions in the two war years, FY 1953 and FY 1969, are shown in table 4-VIII, along with a distribution for a recent peacetime year, FY 1965.

TABLE 4–VIII.—Mental group distribution of enlistments and inductions: DOD
[in thousands]

Mental group	FY 1953		FY 1965		FY 1969	
	Number	Percent	Number	Percent	Number	Percent
I	64	7	22	6	48	6
II	214	24	126	31	247	32
III	279	32	196	49	294	38
IV	283	32	56	14	185	23
Adm acceptee .	46	5	2	—	5	1
Total	886	100	402	100	779	100

The proportion of accessions in the top three mental groups was 63 percent in 1953, at the peak of the Korean expansion, and 76 percent in 1969, at the peak of the Vietnam expansion. During the intervening years the proportion in Categories I-III was higher, reflecting the selectivity possible with the draft during peacetime. Another indication of the quality of enlisted personnel is the fraction of voluntary enlistees who are high school graduates. The proportions for 1959 and 1969 are given in table 4-IX.

TABLE 4–IX.—Percentage of voluntary enlistments with high school diplomas

Service	FY 1959	FY 1969
Army	68	69
Navy	60	80
Marine Corps	54	57
Air Force	73	94
Total DOD	65	76

The services argue that they must have high-quality recruits for the following reasons:

1. The machinery of modern warfare requires recruits who have the mental capability to absorb complex technical training.

2. Training costs can be reduced by limiting enlistments to highly qualified individuals even though men with less mental ability could be taught the requisite skills with enough training investment.

3. The disciplinary problems created by men in the lowest mental group contribute to administrative costs and detract from force effectiveness.

4. Given the normal attrition and losses due to non-re-enlistment, the services must have a large fraction of highly qualified recruits to provide the raw material to staff the non-commissioned officer ranks.

Are the services' quality standards too high? Mental standards were raised significantly between 1957 and 1965, when enlistments of individuals in mental group IV

(AFQT scores of 10 to 30) were limited. In late 1965, the Department of Defense initiated the New Standards Program (Project 100,000), which directed the services to accept 100,000 mental group IV enlistments each year. The services complied and also redesigned many training programs to place less emphasis on written and verbal skills and more on manual talents. Experience gained from this program shows that men with lower AFQT scores and less schooling can achieve acceptable levels of performance. Moreover, the new-standards men have not caused appreciably greater disciplinary problems.

In our studies the number of Category IV enlistees has been limited to a maximum of 20 percent in any service. The recommendations for enlisted compensation are therefore designed to provide that a minimum of 80 percent of the accessions be from Categories I through III. In addition, the recommendation in Chapter 5 to expand the use of proficiency pay and to encourage accelerated promotions provides a selective mechanism to help sustain the quality of military personnel. When these are combined with more intensive recruiting and improvements in military personnel management, the services should be able to maintain the high quality of their forces.

CHAPTER 5

Compensation and Management
of Military Personnel

Pay is not the only, and perhaps not even the primary, motivating force for joining or remaining in the military services. A sense of duty, a desire for adventure or travel, society's esteem for military service, a desire for training, the quality of military life and the general conditions of military service—all affect individuals' decisions. Some of these non-pecuniary factors are beyond the control of the services. Others, however, can be controlled, and the Commission is recommending a number of changes in military manpower procurement and management practices to improve the non-monetary conditions of military life and thereby help increase the attractiveness of military careers. These steps will contribute to the attainment of an all-volunteer force, but are not sufficient in themselves. Military compensation in the early years of service is now so low that it will not sustain an all-volunteer force of the quality desired. Until that condition is corrected, an all-volunteer force cannot be realized.

Our studies show that the increments in pay, and therefore the incremental budgetary outlays, necessary to provide a voluntary force in the 1970's of about the same size as our pre-Vietnam force are fairly small; that they are, in fact, only about as great as those that are required to correct the inequities that have developed in the structure of military compensation during the 21 years that the draft has been in effect.

TABLE 5–I.—Number of volunteers on pre-Vietnam and Vietnam active duty
[thousands]

June 30, 1965

	All services combined			Army only		
	Total [4]	Officers	Enlisted	Total	Officers	Enlisted
All first-term personnel [1]	1,357	92	1,265	560	31	529
Other personnel	1,286	247	1,040	407	81	326
Total active-duty personnel	2,644	339	2,305	967	112	855
Numbers of true volunteers in first-term forces [2] ..	768	54	714	245	18	227
Total number of volunteers [3]	2,054	301	1,754	652	99	553
Percentage of volunteers in the total active-duty forces	77.7	88.7	76.1	67.4	88.0	64.7

Footnotes are found at the end of the table.

TABLE 5-I.—Continued
Number of volunteers on pre-Vietnam and Vietnam active duty
[thousands]

June 30, 1967

All first-term personnel [1]	2,100	126	1,974	1,022	53	968
Other personnel	1,265	259	1,006	418	90	328
Total active-duty personnel	3,365	384	2,981	1,440	144	1,297
Numbers of true volunteers in first-term forces [2]	819	53	766	291	22	269
Total number of volunteers [3]	2,084	312	1,772	710	112	598
Percentage of volunteers in the total active-duty forces [4]	61.9	81.1	59.5	49.3	78.2	46.1

[1] First-term personnel have been defined as those serving their initial obligated tour of duty. In the case of officers, they include regular officers in all branches in their first 4 years of service and non-regular officers serving their first 2 years in the Army and Marine Corps, their first 3 years in the Navy, and 4 years in the Air Force. In the case of enlisted men, first-term regular personnel include those in the first 3 years of service in the Army, 3½ years in the Navy, and 4 years in the Marine Corps and Air Force. Non-regular first-term enlisted personnel are those serving in their first 2 years in all branches of the military.

[2] The number of volunteers in the first-term forces was estimated with the aid of attitude surveys conducted by the Department of Defense. In these surveys, taken in 1964 and 1968, first-term personnel were asked whether they would have enlisted in the absence of a draft. The proportion of respondents who answered "yes" and "probably yes" as opposed to "no" and "probably no" who entered in the year of the survey was applied to the first-term force. The data for 1965 have been adjusted with the factors from the 1964 survey, while those for 1967 were adjusted on the basis of the 1968 survey.

[3] This number is the sum of all those beyond their initial service obligation plus the fraction of true volunteers in the first-term forces.

[4] The differences between totals and the sum of the other entries are due to rounding.

The increase in military compensation that is required to sustain an all-volunteer force of any given size depends upon three factors: (a) the number of accessions that will be needed each year, (b) the number of truly voluntary accessions that are forthcoming at current levels of pay, and (c) the extent to which increases in compensation increase the flow of volunteers. The annual flow of accessions required to maintain the projected all-volunteer forces was discussed in Chapter 4. The extent of voluntarism in the present force is summarized in table 5-I. The next to the last line of table 5-I shows that even under the extremely low levels of entry pay that prevailed in the pre-Vietnam period, the vast majority of those in the then current active duty forces were true volunteers (2.1 of the 2.6 million or about 77 percent of the total force were true volunteers). Indeed, the estimated number of true volunteers even in the Vietnam period (2.1 million) represents a significant fraction of any of the four projected forces the Commission has considered.

The number of volunteers in table 5-I suggests that the forces under study can be attained on a voluntary basis. However, the data also show that unless pay is increased, there will be shortfalls in first-term enlistments, particularly in the Army. For instance, in 1965, true volunteers constituted 76 percent of the total DOD enlisted forces. In the Army, however, only 65 percent of enlisted men were true volunteers.

For a stable force of pre-Vietnam size, the remaining 35 percent of Army enlisted men (either draftees or draft-induced volunteers) could have been replaced by true volunteers, through increasing voluntary enlistments by about 51,000 men per year. Similarly, the entire armed forces in 1965 could have been put on a voluntary basis by adding about 4,000 officer and 84,000 enlisted true volunteers per year. As discussed in Chapter 4, smaller forces would actually require even fewer additional true volunteers. With a continuously rising population 17 to 21 years of age, the task of providing these additional volunteers is not insurmountable.

The problem of attracting more officer volunteers is discussed in detail in Chapter 6. It is important to note here that the shortfall of officer volunteers is small—especially in view of the discrimination which has prevailed in the treatment of pay for first-term officers. Between 1948 and 1965, or between the year the post–World War II draft law was first passed and the most recent peacetime year, the average basic pay of officers with two or more years of military service increased 45 percent while that for officers with less than two years of service increased only about 13 percent.

The history of discrimination against first-term enlisted men is even more striking. During the 1948 to 1965 period the pay of enlisted personnel with two or more years of service increased about 45 percent compared to 4 percent for those with less than two years of service. During the period 1948–1969 the same comparisons show increases of 111 percent and 60 percent respectively. In other words, the basic pay for enlisted recruits increased little more than half as much as that for those with two or more years of service.

Comparisons with civilian pay in table 5-II also point to the relatively low levels of entry pay. Columns 4 and 5 of table 5-II show the ratios of regular and total enlisted and officer compensation to the earnings of their respective civilian counterparts. Although, in general, officers fare relatively better than enlisted men, officer compensation in the first two years of service is below that of comparable civilians. Similarly, based on regular compensation, enlisted pay during the first two years of service is less than 60 percent of comparable civilian pay. Comparisons based on total military and civilian compensation (column 5 of table 5-II) also reveal that enlisted entry pay is significantly below that which the average first-term serviceman would have earned in the civilian economy.

THE EFFECT OF PAY ON RECRUITING AND RETAINING VOLUNTEERS

The data presented in table 5-II suggest the importance of pay as an inducement to enter and remain in the military. For example, the deficits for the officers are smaller than for enlisted personnel. That result is to be expected

TABLE 5-II.—Enlisted men's and comparable civilian compensation profiles by length of service [1970 pay rates][1]

Years of service	Regular military compensation [2]	Total military compensation [3]	Total civilian compensation [4]	Regular military compensation as a percent of total civilian compensation	Total military compensation as a percent of total civilian compensation
1	$ 2,776	$ 3,251	$ 5,202	53.4	62.5
2	3,357	3,935	5,803	57.8	67.8
3	4,496	5,275	6,370	70.6	82.8
4	4,909	6,249	6,908	72.2	90.5
5	5,783	8,516 [5]	7,409	78.1	114.9
6	6,172	8,151	7,876	78.4	103.5
7	6,636	8,741	8,306	79.9	105.2
8	6,845	9,125	8,691	78.8	105.0
9–10	7,242	9,505	9,065	79.9	104.9
11–12	7,715	9,825	9,327	82.7	105.3
13–16	8,290	10,643	9,956	83.3	106.9
17–20	8,964	11,611	10,298	87.0	112.8
21 +	10,483	14,047	10,723	97.8	131.0

Footnotes are found at the end of the table.

TABLE 5–II.—Continued

Officers' and comparable civilian compensation profiles by length of service
[1970 pay rates][1]

Years of service	Regular military compensation [2]	Total military compensation [3]	Total civilian compensation [4]	Regular military compensation as a percent of total civilian compensation	Total military compensation as a percent of total civilian compensation
1	$ 7,337	$ 8,422	$ 8,558	85.7	98.4
2	7,568	8,740	9,291	81.5	94.1
3	9,145	10,732	9,957	91.8	107.8
4	10,906	12,874	10,556	103.3	122.0
5	11,963	14,486	11,089	107.9	130.6
6	12,277	15,050	11,555	106.2	130.2
7	12,779	15,880	12,021	106.3	132.1
8	12,856	16,214	12,488	103.0	129.8
9–10	13,245	16,759	13,243	100.0	126.5
11–12	14,058	18,144	14,689	95.7	123.5
13–16	14,986	19,545	15,844	94.6	123.4
17–20	16,159	21,290	16,470	98.1	129.3
21 +	19,142	26,771	17,765	107.8	150.7

Footnotes on next page.

TABLE 5–II.—Footnotes:

[1] See appendix B below for a discussion of the degree of comparability between the military and the civilian compensation figures recorded in this table.

[2] Regular military compensation is the sum of basic pay, basic allowances for subsistence and quarters, and tax advantage. The two allowances are provided either in cash or in kind. In either case they are non-taxable. The tax advantage is an estimate of the taxes saved by the military personnel but paid by a comparable civilian in order to have the same net compensation. The basic pay rates are those expected to be in effect in late 1970, which are assumed to be 8 percent above those prevailing in July of 1969.

[3] Total military compensation includes, in addition to the regular compensation, the other current cash pays such as bonuses, incentive pay, and specialty pays (except hostile fire pay), as well as the estimated value of future retired pay. It also includes an estimate of the value of such fringe benefits as full medical services for the individual and his family and commissary and post exchange privileges.

[4] The total civilian compensation figures recorded in column (3) are derived from the wages and salaries reported by the Census Bureau's Current Population Survey for 1963, 1964, 1965, and 1966. These earnings were converted to 1966 dollars, were smoothed somewhat to reduce sampling error, and were adjusted by a factor of 1.226 to take account of the pay raises between 1966 and 1970. In addition, the reported earnings were raised by 8.6 percent to take account of the employer's contributions to such fringe benefits as are included in the total military compensation figures. The 8.6 percent figure is based on the 1967 Civilian Fringe Benefit data reported by the U.S. Chamber of Commerce. The civilian compensation figures that are being compared with the compensation figures for enlisted personnel are those for white high-school graduates aged 19, 20, 21, and so on, while the figures used for the officer comparison are those for white college graduates, 16 years of education or more, aged 23, 24, 25, and so on. It is assumed here that the average enlisted man enters military service at age 19 and the average officer begins his career at age 23.

[5] Total military compensation is higher in year 5 than in the subsequent 2 years of service because it includes the regular re-enlistment bonus that is given in lump sum form at the point of re-enlistment.

given that officer entry pay is relatively higher than enlisted entry pay. Voluntary enlisted deficits are highest in the Army. This result, too, is to be expected, given that entry level pay is lowest for enlisted personnel and that the non-monetary conditions of service are less attractive in the Army than in the other three military services.

In addition to this indirect evidence, we have used several methods to estimate directly the effect of increases in first- and second-term pay on voluntary enlistments and re-enlistments. Based on these studies, and on the observed impact on retention of proficiency pay and the variable re-enlistment bonus, we estimate that a 10 percent increase in the current value of first-term regular military compensation will result in an increase of about 12.5 percent in the voluntary enlistment rate from the 17 to 21 year old civilian population. In the case of the Army, a 40 percent pay raise would increase the voluntary enlistment rate from about 1.388 to about 2.079 per 100 men in the 17 to 21 age cohort. The same percentage increase in officer compensation will induce a roughly comparable rise in the voluntary enlistment rate from the college population.

The Commission's compensation recommendations are designed both to eliminate past inequities and to assure the services a flow of enlistments of the quantity and quality that will be required to maintain a base force of about 2.5 million men and women. Smaller forces could be maintained with smaller increments in pay, while larger forces would require a larger increase in pay.

The Commission has made two kinds of pay recommendations, those requiring implementation prior to or concomitant with the transition to an all-volunteer force, and those equally necessary for reasons of equity and efficiency, but not essential to the achievement of an all-volunteer force. In the former category are increased basic pay, the extension of skill differentials to the first-term population, and an increase in hostile fire pay. In the latter category are the development of a military salary system comparable to that in the civilian sector, including the substitution of cash for some benefits that are now provided in-kind, and the modification of the present retirement system, including the introduction of vesting.

Basic Pay

The recommended increases in basic pay are designed to provide the Army with the quantity and quality of volunteers required for an overall force level of approximately 2.5 million men. The evidence is overwhelming that, if compensation is set at levels which satisfy Army requirements, the other services will be able to attract enough qualified volunteers to meet their respective requirements.

The Commission urges that its recommendations be enacted with a minimum of delay and recommends an effective date of July 1, 1970. Since there is a good chance that civil service and military pay will also increase during fiscal 1971, we have assumed a basic pay increase of 8 percent on July 1, 1970, for all military personnel. The pay rates in table 5-III reflect a combination of that across-the-board increase with the recommended pay raises designed to achieve an all-volunteer force of 2.5 million men. The latter increase raises the current value of enlisted basic pay during the first term of service by about 50 percent. The recommended increase for those in their second term of service is about 9 percent. Officers in their first 3 years of service receive a 28 percent basic pay raise.

Table 5-III shows that these recommended increases merely "straighten" the regular military compensation line; they give individuals in their initial years of service about the same pay relative to civilian compensation as the career force receives. These pay raises for first-term personnel are justified on equity grounds alone.

This recommended pay increase will add $2.68 billion to the budget in fiscal year 1971, but this added outlay will be smaller in future years if forces decline to the 2.5-million-man level and, also, as a result of the further manpower reduction produced by lower turnover in the all-volunteer force which will decrease the force strengths required to provide a given level of defense capability (see chapter 4). Since military pay is either high or low only in relation to civilian earnings, annual adjustments in military pay will be necessary to ensure that they remain competitive.

The pay recommendations incorporated in table 5-III are intended to apply to the 2.0, 2.25, and 2.5 million forces, but they are actually in excess of those required for either the 2- or 2.25-million-man forces. Indeed, the figures in table 5-I suggest that no pay increase is required to provide an all-volunteer force of 2 million men and that a relatively small increase over current levels is required to induce the additional volunteers necessary for a 2.25-million-man force. The Commission recommends this pay raise for all three of the above named forces on equity grounds alone. The 3.0-million-man all-volunteer force will require a pay increase above that shown in table 5-III. The extra increase required for the 3-million-man force would add $2.21 billion more to the budget in the years 1977–1979.

Skill Differentials

The basic pay recommendations in table 5-III are designed to cover the majority of the enlisted force. However, the armed forces must attract some persons with special skills or unusual aptitudes. The military services have the authority to offer higher pay to such individuals by offering higher grades when they enter service or by increasing the speed of promotion. To some extent both of these practices are being followed by the services. These practices should be broadened and formalized, to make military careers more attractive to high quality personnel.

To ensure further the maintenance of the quality of military personnel, proficiency pay should be made available to those in critical occupations after the satisfactory completion of advanced training. Currently, proficiency pay is available only to those in the career force. These recommendations should enable the services to satisfy their needs for exceptional personnel. It is estimated that an additional $214 million per year will be required to cover the expenditures for this purpose.

Hostile Fire Pay

Military service demands a high degree of personal commitment and exposes most servicemen to risks and

TABLE 5-III.—Recommended pay profiles for enlisted personnel for July 1, 1970

Years of service	Regular military compensation [1]	Total military compensation [2]	Regular military compensation as a percent of total civilian compensation [3]	Total military compensation as a percent of total civilian compensation
1	$ 4,498	$ 5,041	86.5	96.9
2	4,917	5,631	84.7	97.0
3	5,311	6,237	83.4	97.9
4	5,735	7,195	83.0	104.2
5	6,143	9,131 [4]	82.9	123.2
6	6,530	8,597	82.9	109.2
7	6,880	9,055	82.8	109.0
8	7,203	9,582	82.9	110.3
9–10	7,510	9,838	82.8	108.5
11–12	7,721	9,745	82.8	104.5
13–16	8,296	10,550	83.3	106.0
17–20	8,969	11,616	87.1	112.8
21 +	10,489	14,053	97.8	131.1

Footnotes are found at the end of the table.

TABLE 5–III.—Continued
Recommended pay profiles for officers for July 1, 1970

Years of service	Regular military compensation [1]	Total military compensation [2]	Regular military compensation as a percent of total civilian compensation [3]	Total military compensation as a percent of total civilian compensation
1	$ 8,868	$ 9,952	103.6	116.3
2	9,635	10,808	103.7	116.3
3	10,315	11,902	103.6	119.5
4	10,923	12,885	103.5	122.1
5	11,999	14,520	108.2	130.9
6	12,313	15,077	106.6	130.5
7	12,810	15,897	106.6	132.2
8	12,890	16,243	103.2	130.1
9–10	13,271	16,756	100.2	126.5
11–12	14,080	18,128	95.6	123.4
13–16	15,008	19,534	94.7	123.3
17–20	16,192	21,293	98.3	129.3
21 +	19,168	26,757	107.9	150.6

[1], [2], and [3]: See footnotes [2], [3], and [4] respectively of table 5–II for the definitions of regular military compensation, total military compensation, and total civilian compensation.

[4] See footnote [5] of table 5–II.

hardships that are generally greater than those found in the civilian economy. Beyond that, a small fraction of the military force is sometimes required to serve under conditions of risk to life and limb that are not only greater than those faced by most service personnel, but exceptionally high even among those serving in a combat zone.

As a matter of equity as well as to provide compensation flexibility in conflict situations, the Commission recommends that a new and higher maximum level of hostile fire pay of $200 per month be enacted. Eligibility for this maximum level of hazardous duty pay should be restricted to those who in the course of their duties are regularly exposed to hostile fire and only for the period of such exposure. The current levels of hazardous duty pay should be provided to others in the combat zone who take higher than normal risks but are not regularly exposed to hostile fire.

Since the specific number of individuals who will serve under such extreme hazardous conditions is likely to be small, we have not estimated the budgetary implications of this proposal.

Development of a Military Salary System of Pay

Military pay today is a conglomeration of current and future pay and benefits that are difficult to enumerate and even more difficult to measure and evaluate. Military pay lacks visibility. It functions as a continuous source of controversy. It is inequitable. It is inefficient in attracting and retaining desired personnel.

All of these deficiencies, and especially the last two, result from the different ways of paying individuals performing the same task, and from the large proportion of pay that is provided either in-kind or as retirement income. This in-kind and deferred compensation has little value for a new recruit or a first-term serviceman trying to decide whether to re-enlist.

Recognizing these defects, a Department of Defense study group recommended the introduction of a "salary" system of pay in which allowances for quarters and subsistence would have been combined with basic pay to provide a "salary." The Commission supports this recommendation.

Retirement Vesting

Because military retirement benefits are budgeted each year out of current funds, servicemen have never acquired vested retirement rights except those which arise after one has served long enough (19½ years) to be eligible to retire. This policy has a number of undesirable effects.

First, because retired pay is deferred it has little value for an individual in his early years of service, even if he is seriously considering a military career. It is worth nothing to the serviceman who does not plan to make the military a career. Yet, the armed forces need both non-career and career personnel.

Retirement benefits have the additional disadvantage of being worth too much to the individual who is beyond his tenth or eleventh year of service. He cannot afford to separate from the service because of the benefits for which he will qualify after another 9 or 10 years. Because of this potential loss, the military rarely discharges individuals who have served more than, say, 10 years.

Also, the substantial retirement income available after 20 years of service (when some enlisted men are only 37 years old) induces many individuals to retire as soon as they are eligible. The combination of retirement income and civilian earnings is very attractive. Men who retire early are often those with superior civilian earning opportunities and they are precisely the individuals the services would like to retain longer. The Department of Defense group organized to study compensation recognized the shortcomings of the present retirement system. They recommended increasing military pay sufficiently to enable military personnel to contribute 6½ percent of their salaries annually to their retirement account without any loss in net income, the introduction of partial vesting after 5 years of service, and a reduction in the retirement income available in the years prior to the normal retirement age. The recommendations incorporated provisions to ensure that those who entered the services under the old retirement system would suffer no loss.

The Commission supports these recommendations regarding retirement benefits. The Commission also believes that it would be equitable and desirable to give officers and enlisted men the same vested retirement rights as civil service employees currently have.

Compensation-in-Kind and Fringe Benefits

Many recommendations have been made for increasing military compensation-in-kind including improved housing, educational programs, dental care for dependents, etc. The quality of military life needs to be improved generally, and such programs would surely contribute to that end.

Nevertheless, we have decided against recommending general increases in such benefits or in income-in-kind items of pay. We have done so because the military pay package already has a substantially larger proportion of such items than is found in the civilian sector of the economy and because we believe that general increases in non-cash pay would be an inefficient means of compensating military personnel.

Funds that are used to construct and maintain housing can also be used to increase basic pay, and funds to sponsor educational programs can be used to provide dental care for dependents. Thus, the question is not whether such benefits are desirable, but whether they are the most effective form of compensation. Providing compensation in cash has an inherent advantage in that context—it allows each individual to decide how he or she will use whatever he earns. He can thus get the full value of whatever costs are incurred by the government in paying him. When he is compensated in non-cash form, however, the value of what he receives is often less to him than its cost to the government. Meanwhile, he is encouraged to consume more of particular goods or services than he otherwise would. Non-cash pay also tends to result in inefficient patterns of compensation by favoring some individuals (heavy users of these items) over others, independent of performance. For example, most military non-cash pay is of little value to young men and women. Therefore it is not very effective in helping to attract and retain new personnel. Finally, as was learned in the Defense Department study, the effect of non-cash remuneration on enlistments and retentions is attenuated because such compensation is not very visible. While compensation-in-kind is sometimes justifiable for tax reasons in the civilian economy, that reason does not apply to military compensation since the government is both payer of the cash compensation and recipient of whatever taxes are collected.

However, special circumstances in the military often warrant pay-in-kind. At remote bases, housing and other services often would not be available unless provided under military auspices, and in many instances, military personnel are required to live on base. Under such circumstances accommodations and services should be made attractive and efficient so as to enhance the conditions of military life.

MANAGEMENT OF MILITARY PERSONNEL

The Commission believes that in addition to the recommendations above there are several opportunities available to increase voluntarism, particularly among higher quality personnel, by improving the conditions of military service and the quality of military life.

Terms of Enlistment

One of the conditions of military service that distinguishes it from civilian employment is the practice of requiring enlisted personnel to obligate themselves for specific limited terms of service. An enlisted man is required periodically to declare his intentions to remain in the military, and he is permitted to resign only when he reaches such a decision point. We believe that this policy is not necessary, and that it adversely affects the attractiveness of military service. We recommend elimination of the present system of obligated terms of service so that enlisted personnel would be recruited and retained on the same basis as commissioned officers. Within the limits prescribed below this means that enlisted men would generally be granted discharges upon request.

The right of enlisted men to a discharge should be limited in the following ways:

(a) The Defense Department should have the authority to deny such discharges in an emergency, just as it does with officers.

(b) Enlisted men should be obligated to fulfill terms of service commensurate with the cost of the training they receive. This should apply not only to new recruits, but also to those receiving advanced training. The Defense Department should undertake a study to determine the length of obligated service to be required for various training programs. Such a study would specify a minimum term of service for new recruits. We do not contemplate that it would be reasonable to require terms of service of less than approximately two years for recruits.

(c) The Defense Department should have the right to deny discharges to enlisted personnel who have received orders for overseas duty or sea duty.

If the Defense Department adopts this policy as to obligated terms of service, the services should simultaneously establish procedures for periodic reviews designed to identify and separate servicemen who are not performing satisfactorily.

Though this change may appear dramatic, the abandonment of the present system of fixed enlistment terms should not create serious problems for the military. Such a system has not harmed the officer corps. The increased freedom of choice should make military service more attractive and enhance the dignity of an enlisted career.

Choice of Military Occupation

The Commission recommends an expansion of the current program whereby enlistees are permitted to specify their choice of occupation as a condition of enlistment. Such a policy should increase the efficiency of manpower utilization within the military and, also, by reducing the uncertainty of military life, increase the attractiveness of a military career.

The Commission believes that expansion of the existing

program will not weaken the services' ability to fulfill their mission, even though it may increase somewhat the cost of managing the recruitment facilities. The services do not appear to have experienced any ill effects from their present policy of giving individuals a choice of their service branch and, to a large extent, their occupational field.

Lateral Hiring

Many of the functions performed in a modern military organization have parallels in the civilian economy, for example, construction, supply and logistics, personnel management, equipment and facilities maintenance, research and development, and medical service. With minor exceptions the officers and the enlisted personnel who staff these functions in the military are products of the military personnel system. They enter the service as untrained recruits, take basic and advanced formal or on-the-job training, and acquire the experience necessary to function effectively while on a military assignment. The similarity between military and civilian functions, however, suggests that military positions might in many instances be filled by already skilled individuals who transfer from the civilian economy.

Lateral hiring—the hiring of skilled personnel into the armed services at pay grades commensurate with their training and experience—offers the services an opportunity to enlarge the manpower pool from which they draw. In the past they have resorted to lateral hiring to procure personnel with special skills. During World War II the practice was used extensively, not only for enlisted personnel, but also for officers. Also, the military has consistently permitted doctors, dentists, and lawyers to enter the services at officer ranks above the usual entry level.

Currently, the largest enlisted lateral hiring program is the Navy's "Direct Petty Officer Procurement Program," which has been used since 1965 to man Naval construction battalions. Under this revival of the World War II Seabee program over 5,000 civilian construction workers have been hired into pay grades E4 through E7 with a service obligation of two and one-half years. The program is apparently a success. Draft pressure, higher pay, and the shorter service obligation (two and one-half rather than the normal four years) have allowed the Navy to be highly selective.

The Army has used lateral hiring to recruit medical and dental technicians at entry pay grades of E4 and E5. Each lateral enlistee receives about 16 weeks of basic and advanced training. The Army also plans to introduce a program for selected engineer occupational fields which are significantly undermanned.

These examples, however, are the exception rather than the rule. On balance, the services have used lateral hiring sparingly. At worst they have limited the payment of re-enlistment bonuses to those who re-enlist within six months of discharge so that a qualified trained veteran who has been out longer is offered no special incentive to return.

There are, of course, inherent limits to lateral entry. Not all military occupations have civilian counterparts, and even where such counterparts exist it may be less costly for the military to provide the training and experience. Notwithstanding the limiting considerations, the military are sacrificing an important opportunity by severely restricting the use of lateral entry. Moreover, lateral entry would help dissolve the barrier which some feel separates the military from civilian society.

Entitlements

At present, enlisted men who are not E4's with four or more years of service are not entitled to dislocation allowance and reimbursement of family travel expense when they are ordered to a new duty station. This discrimination imposes an unnecessary hardship on first-term servicemen. The Commission recommends that entitlement to reimbursement of family travel expense and dislocation allowance be extended to all enlisted personnel.

CHAPTER 6

Officer Procurement and Retention

Regardless of the type of procurement system used, the officer corps is a crucial element in the effectiveness of any military establishment. An all-volunteer armed force must attract an adequate supply of officers from the limited number of individuals in the population who possess the necessary leadership qualities and motivation.

In recent years the major portion of the officer corps has been recruited from the ranks of college graduates. While it is important to continue to attract college-graduate officers, the decision to staff the officer corps almost entirely with college graduates was somewhat arbitrary and came about in part because of the favorable recruiting climate provided by the draft. Without the draft, a college-graduate officer corps will be more difficult to recruit and will require higher pay levels than one which includes some non-college graduates. To balance the need for high-quality officers with the extra cost that a voluntary all-college graduate force will entail, we assume in our estimates that about 90 percent of the officers entering the service each year will be college graduates. It is expected that most non-college graduates will either have graduated from two-year college programs or have at least two years of college.

Staffing the non-specialist portion of the officer corps in an all-volunteer armed force will be somewhat easier than recruiting the enlisted force. Two main reasons underlie our optimism. First, except during the Vietnam escalation of recent years, little difficulty has been encountered in recruiting new officers from among college graduates.

While the draft has been an important positive factor in this recruiting, the flow of volunteers has been impressive in view of the relative ease with which college graduates could avoid military service through the middle 1960's.[1] Also to be taken into account is the relatively large proportion of first-term officers who remain in the military beyond their obligated period of service. Over 70 percent of officer personnel are currently beyond their obligated period of service and, therefore, can be considered career officers.

The second reason for optimism stems from the large and growing pool of educationally qualified young men who will be available in the 1970's for military service as officers. Since 1960, the number of male college graduates has grown from 230,000 per year to 390,000 per year—an increase of 70 percent. By 1980, this number will increase 25 percent more to 490,000 annually.[2] With an armed force of 2.5 million, the annual requirement for new officers is not likely to exceed 30,000. This number can be met by recruiting about 7 percent of the yearly graduating classes of U.S. colleges and universities in the mid-1970's.

PROCUREMENT

Most commissioned officer procurement programs are designed chiefly to attract college graduates. These sources of officers can be divided into four major groups: Reserve Officer Training Corps (ROTC) and other in-college programs, Officer Candidate programs, service academies, and direct appointments. In addition, there are a number of programs which provide Warrant Officers, Limited Duty Officers, and Temporary Officers. By and large this range of programs has met the needs of the services even when these have changed rather drastically. The same major programs, perhaps modified in form, can be ex-

---

[1] Of those males reaching 26 years of age in 1964, 40 percent of the college graduates served in some capacity in the armed forces; many in the 4 to 6 month reserve program. In comparison, over 55 percent of those who did not continue their education past high school, and 60 percent of those with some college served. For those with less than a high school diploma the rate was 50 percent.

[2] Derived from U.S. Department of Health, Education and Welfare, Office of Education, *Earned Degrees Conferred by Institutions of Higher Education.*

pected to supply the bulk of new officers in an all-volunteer armed force.

Reserve Officer Training Corps (ROTC) and Other College Programs

By far the largest single source of newly commissioned officers is the Reserve Officer Training Corps. Designed primarily for four-year colleges, it accounted for 26 percent of all new officers in the period just preceding the Vietnam War. (See table 6-I.) An additional 15 percent of officers commissioned in FY 1965 were obtained from a variety of in-college programs. Chief among these are the Reserve Officer Corps (ROC) in the Navy and the Platoon Leader Corps (PLC) in the Marine Corps. The major distinction between these programs and the ROTC program is that military training is provided entirely during the summer at special training centers run by the military, whereas the ROTC cadet receives a major portion of his training at his university during the school year. Because of the long lead time—two to four years—required for increasing the supply of officers from these sources, their relative importance declined during the rapid troop build-up in the early stages of the Vietnam War.

The importance of ROTC officers varies considerably from service to service. In FY 1965, they accounted for about 60 percent of newly commissioned Army officers, slightly less than 35 percent of new Air Force officers, and less than 15 percent of new Navy officers. In the Marine Corps only about 7 percent of the new officers were commissioned through the Navy-run ROTC program. The great majority of Marine officers were recruited from the PLC program.

At the completion of an ROTC student's college education he is required to serve a minimum term of obligated service. This minimum currently varies from service to service and according to the type of program. All scholarship recipients, regardless of service, must serve four years of active duty. For non-scholarship holders, the minimum is two years in the Army, three in the Navy and Marine Corps, and four in the Air Force. The two-

TABLE 6–I.—Officer accessions by service and source of commission: selected years, 1960, 1965, 1968

	FY 1960 Number	FY 1960 Percent*	FY 1965 Number	FY 1965 Percent*	FY 1968 Number	FY 1968 Percent*
Total all services:						
Academies	1,546	5.0	1,896	4.7	2,131	3.0
ROTC and other college programs [1]	13,267	43.1	16,697	41.4	18,305	26.1
OCS	3,615	11.7	9,499	23.6	18,753	**26.7
Non-college graduate programs	3,464	11.2	1,454	3.6	13,874	***19.8
Ad. from reserves	743	2.4	1,169	2.9	4,527	6.5
Direct appointment (medical) [2]	4,605	15.0	5,178	12.9	7,602	10.8
All others [3]	3,526	11.5	4,430	10.9	4,936	7.0
Total	30,766	100.0	40,322	100.0	70,128	100.0
Army:						
Academy	503	4.9	524	3.2	677	1.9
ROTC	6,252	60.8	9,886	60.5	10,176	28.1
OCS	—	—	1,527	9.3	4,398	12.1
Non-college graduate programs	729	7.1	750	4.6	13,733	**37.9
Ad. from reserves	525	5.1	595	3.6	1,517	4.2
Direct appointment (medical) [2]	1,418	13.8	1,664	10.2	3,123	8.6
All others [3]	850	8.2	1,392	8.6	2,590	7.1
Total	10,277	100.0	16,338	100.0	36,214	100.0

Footnotes are found at the end of the table.

TABLE 6-I.—Officer accessions by service and source of commission: selected years, 1960, 1965, 1968.—Continued

	FY 1960		FY 1965		FY 1968	
	Number	Percent *	Number	Percent *	Number	Percent *
Navy:						
Academy	648	6.9	714	6.5	744	6.0
ROTC and other college programs [1]	2,149	23.0	1,859	16.9	1,916	15.3
OCS	2,852	30.5	3,877	35.3	6,128	48.8
Non-college graduate programs	522	5.6	361	3.3	58	.5
Ad. from reserves	110	1.2	515	4.7	811	6.5
Direct appointment (medical) [2]	1,038	11.1	966	8.8	2,013	16.0
All others [3]	2,041	21.8	2,678	24.2	882	7.0
Total	9,360	100.0	10,970	100.0	12,552	100.0
Marine Corps:						
Academy	70	.4	78	4.0	86	2.3
ROTC and other college programs [1]	888	49.4	1,116	56.5	1,221	33.0
OCS (OCC)	441	24.6	439	22.2	1,944	***52.5
Non-college graduate programs	183	10.2	184	9.3	83	2.2
Ad. from reserves	108	.6	59	3.0	127	3.4
Direct appointment	—	—	—	—	—	—
All others [3]	106	.6	98	4.9	243	6.6
Total	1,796	100.0	1,974	100.0	3,074	100.0

Footnotes are found at the end of the table.

TABLE 6–I.—Officer accessions by service and source of commission: selected years, 1960, 1965, 1968.—Continued

	FY 1960		FY 1965		FY 1968	
	Number	Percent*	Number	Percent*	Number	Percent*
Air Force:						
Academy	325	3.5	579	5.3	624	3.5
ROTC	3,978	42.6	3,836	34.7	4,992	28.3
OCS (OTS)	322	3.4	3,656	33.1	6,283	35.6
Non-college graduate programs	2,030	21.7	159	1.4	2,072	11.7
Ad. from reserves	—	—	—	—	2,466	14.0
Direct appointment (medical) [2]	2,149	23.0	2,548	23.1		
All others [3]	529	5.7	262	2.4	1,221	6.9
Total	9,333	100.0	11,040	100.0	17,658	100.0

* Detail does not add to total.
** Includes many college graduates who entered OCS after enlisting or being drafted.
*** Includes 2-year college graduates as well as some with no college degree.

[1] Includes Reserve Officer Corps graduates in the Navy and Platoon Leader graduates in Marine Corps.

[2] Includes physicians, dentists, and veterinarians.

[3] Comprises primarily professional appointment, including lawyers and other medical specialists. Also includes women officers and nurses. For the Navy and Marine Corps a variety of commissioning programs from the enlisted ranks is included.

year Army obligation was in part designed to be consistent with the active duty obligation of a draftee. We have assumed in our projections that in a voluntary force the minimum Army ROTC obligation will be three years.

During the last few years, a number of schools either ended their ROTC programs, or indicated they planned to do so in the near future. While it is not clear whether these are isolated events or the beginning of a trend, there is little doubt that some type of college recruiting program will continue in the future. For planning purposes, we assumed that ROTC will continue to be the major source of new officers for the Army and Air Force. The problem of declining ROTC enrollment is discussed later in the chapter.

A number of Department of Defense studies have recently been undertaken concerning the future of ROTC. While differing somewhat in goals and procedures, all recommend an increase in the number of ROTC college scholarships. We endorse this recommendation and encourage the use of such scholarships as a way of attracting applicants not likely to enter the program without them—especially those whose skills or aptitudes are in short supply in the military. In our projections of potential officer supply without a draft, we assumed an increase of 4,500 scholarships a year for each service (Marine Corps included in Navy total) producing 1,000 additional ROTC officers a year per service (see table 6-II). The total cost of such a program will be between $25 and $30 million per year and is included in our estimates of the increased budgetary expenditures associated with the creation of an all-volunteer officers corps.

With an all-volunteer armed force, one must expect that fewer students will volunteer for ROTC training, particularly in the first two years. Hence many schools may find that they can no longer operate viable programs. To insure that ROTC instruction remains available to interested students, it may be advisable in the future to establish area training centers. Thus students from a number of schools in one geographic region could participate in the same training program.

Serious consideration should also be given to the increased use of scholarship and non-scholarship Reserve

TABLE 6-II.—Army commissioned officer requirements and potential supply in an all-volunteer force
[2.5 million man force level]

Fiscal Year	Potential supply						Total	Required accessions	Estimated surplus or shortage
	ROTC				OCS				
	Academy [1]	Scholarship [2]	Non-scholarship [3]	College graduates [4]	Non-college graduates [5]	Others [6]			
1971	900	1,400	11,200	200	1,000	1,400	16,100	16,800	— 700
1972	900	1,500	8,000	300	1,000	500	12,200	5,300	+6,900
1973	1,000	2,000	5,700	300	1,000	600	10,600	7,100	+3,500
1974	1,000	2,500	3,200	400	1,000	1,000	9,100	11,400	—2,300
1975	1,000	2,500	3,100	500	1,000	700	8,800	8,700	+ 100
1976	1,000	2,500	4,100	500	1,000	700	9,800	8,500	+1,300
1977	1,000	2,500	5,100	500	1,000	800	10,900	9,900	+1,000
1978	1,000	2,500	6,000	600	1,000	800	11,900	9,500	+2,400
1979	1,000	2,500	6,800	600	1,000	800	12,700	9,000	+3,700
1980	1,000	2,500	7,300	600	1,000	800	13,200	9,400	+3,800

Note: Numbers rounded to nearest hundred.

[1] Based on current Army plans.

[2] Assumes an increase in current Army plans of 500 in 1973 and 1,000 thereafter.

[3] Assumes the additional 1,000 ROTC scholarships are given to new applicants and are not included in ROTC projections (original 1,500 were assumed to be included).

[4] Assumes growth in 1964 proportion of college graduates entering OCS in line with estimated growth in male college population adjusted for the war-induced decline in the rate estimated from ROTC. Estimated proportion of draft-induced volunteers among 1964 entrants equals 60 percent.

[5] Assumes approximately 10 percent of officer entrants will be non-college graduates.

[6] Includes mostly direct appointments and entrants from special commissioning programs. Ratio of such officer to total requirements instituted at prewar level.

Officer Corps and Platoon Leader Corps-type programs. Unlike the present ROTC, such programs do not require the stationing of permanent units on a great many campuses. With the introduction of an all-volunteer force and the reduction in the size of each ROTC unit, the per-graduate expense is likely to rise. If much of the military training can be provided during the summer in training stations which receive applicants from many schools, there is a good possibility that substantial savings can be realized.

Officer Candidate Programs

While officer candidate programs were originally established to train officers recruited from the enlisted ranks, they have increasingly been used in recent years to supplement the flow of new college graduates into the officer corps. The large demand for new officers created by the Vietnam buildup, however, required the Army, in particular, to allow significant numbers of non-college graduates to enter its OCS program. Officer Candidate Schools programs are more responsive than ROTC to changes in military requirements, requiring a lead time of three to nine months as opposed to two to four years for the ROTC. With an all-volunteer force, each service will require more flexibility in the recruiting of officers. In addition to new college graduates, the services will doubtless seek to attract somewhat older civilians who desire to enter one of the more specialized and less physically demanding branches of the military. Such volunteers will require some military training, which is likely to be most efficiently provided through OCS-type programs.

Academies

A small but highly important number of new officers are commissioned annually by the service academies. Ranging in size from about 3 percent of the annual number of entering officers in the Army to more than 6 percent in the Navy, academy graduates form an important component of each service's officer corps. Their high career motivation is clearly shown by the fact that upon completion of their obligated tour of active duty (now

5 years), between 80 and 90 percent can be expected to remain in the service, as opposed to less than 50 percent for ROTC scholarship graduates and under 25 percent for OCS graduates.

With the planned expansion of the U.S. Military Academy and the Air Force Academy, academy graduates in 1973 will number about 2,840. For the foreseeable future, even with an all-volunteer force, we do not anticipate a need to increase further the size of the academies. Such expansion would be very costly and it is also highly desirable that military officers continue to be recruited from a wide range of civilian colleges and universities.

Direct Commissioning Programs

Each service requires many individuals possessing non-combat-type skills available in the civilian population. These include chaplains, lawyers, physicians, dentists, and specially trained technicians. Because of the importance and special problems connected with the recruitment of physicians, a separate study was undertaken by the Commission. The highlights of this study are reported in Chapter 8. By and large, because appointment officers perform the same tasks in the military as in the civilian sector, they usually receive no extra military training. Such direct appointments have accounted for about 20 percent of new officers each year.

Since a major portion of these officers would not have entered military service without the draft, an all-volunteer force will necessitate more in-service training and further increases in the substitution of civilians for military personnel. In addition, we would suggest that procedures be established to attract civilians who already possess the necessary training, by offering advanced officer grades Such lateral hiring generally should be limited to those specialties which require an individual to possess technical skills learned in the civilian sector and to those tasks and functions which must be performed by a military officer.

Warrant, Limited Duty, and Temporary Officers

Each service includes men who hold the rank of officer but who are not considered part of the regular commissioned officer corps. Included in this group are Warrant Officers, Limited Duty Officers, and Temporary Officers. Such ranks are designed for non-college graduates who occupy positions which require greater technical skills and carry larger responsibilities than the enlisted grades. In most instances, such officer ranks are awarded to superior enlisted personnel. The Army, however, actively recruits civilian two-year college graduates and men with some college for their helicopter pilot warrant officer program.

The increased availability of four-year college graduates during the 1960's resulted in a decline in the use of these programs. Expanded officer requirements during the Vietnam buildup have reversed this trend. To facilitate the transition to, and the maintenance of, an all-volunteer armed force, we assumed in our analysis that greater use will be made of these sources of officer manpower.

Projected Supply of Army Officers in an All-Volunteer Force

The problem of maintaining a voluntary Officer Corps is more difficult in the Army than it is in the other services. If the level of officer compensation is high enough to meet Army accession requirements, it will also be adequate for the Air Force, Navy, and Marine Corps. For that reason the analysis of officer supply focuses on the Army.

The most important source of supply of Army officers is ROTC. We have derived estimates of the number of Army officers which ROTC will produce in an all-volunteer environment for the period 1971 to 1980, from an analysis of ROTC enrollments at schools where participation is voluntary. These projections are calculated on the assumption that: (1) the draft is ended in 1971; (2) the level of war intensity declines by 1972 to the prebuildup level of 1964; and (3) military pay relative to civilian earnings is increased to comparability, as described in Chapter 5, table 5-III.

The ROTC supply figures are shown in table 6-II along with estimates of supply from the other officer procurement programs. Because of the special benefits inherent in receiving an ROTC scholarship or enrolling in the U.S. Military Academy, we anticipate that both programs will continue to be fully subscribed in an all-volunteer armed force, and will produce the expected number of annual accessions. The technique for estimating output from the other procurement sources is summarized in the footnotes to table 6-I.

The total potential flow of men into the Army Officer Corps will continue at a high level through FY 1972 because of draft-induced volunteers remaining in the pipeline. The lowest level of Army ROTC entrants, we estimate, will be in FY 1975. Most officers commissioned in that year would have entered the ROTC program in 1971—a time when the negative impact of the war on enrollments will probably be at its height. After FY 1975, as the war's impact on past enrollments diminishes and more men enter as a result of the pay raise, potential supply will increase. Except for FY 1974, the estimated supply will be more than adequate to meet anticipated accession requirements to maintain the Army Officer Corps in a 2.5-million-man force without the draft. This one-year shortfall can easily be offset by permitting more accessions in the previous two years. Hence, we feel justified in concluding that the recommended all-volunteer pay profile plus anticipated increases in the ROTC scholarship program will be sufficient to maintain the officer corps for each service at required levels for an all-volunteer armed force of 2.5 million or less. In the late 1970's the supply estimates shown in table 6-II are sufficient to staff the officer corps in a 3.0 million volunteer armed force. To insure that the required number of accessions for such a larger force would be forthcoming, however, we have included in our cost estimates for the 3.0-million-man force a further increase in officer pay.

Retention

In an all-volunteer force, more officers will stay beyond their initial obligated period of service than with a draft. Those who today constitute true volunteers—individuals who would have entered military service without the draft—will make up a larger proportion of first-term officers, and their demonstrated higher retention experience will increase overall first-term retention.

First-term retention in the current force varies considerably from one procurement source to another and from one service to another. For those procurement programs including a large concentration of draft-motivated volunteers, which will not be as important in an all-volunteer force, the proportion remaining beyond the obligated period of service is relatively low. In this category, in particular, are college-graduate OCS officers in the Army and Navy where first-term retention rates are less than 30 percent. At the other end of the spectrum, at least 80 out of every 100 academy graduates can be expected to remain beyond their obligated period of service. Overall, the Air Force has the highest first-term retention rate and the Army, the lowest.

The impact on turnover of eliminating the draft can be appreciated by analyzing the results of a Department of Defense survey of active duty personnel. As shown in table 6-III, among officers serving their original obligated tour of duty, 46 percent of those who indicated they would have entered the military without the draft said they planned to remain on active duty until retirement. Of those who were considered draft-motivated volunteers, only 16 percent said they expected to ramain in the service.

The survey results generally confirm expected differences in retention between services and sources of commission. From all sources of commission, the Army is revealed to have the smallest proportion of career-motivated first-term officers, while the Air Force has the largest. For each service, even among those who were considered to be draft-motivated volunteers, academy graduates consistently record the highest overall expected retention rate. High retention rates are also shown for ROTC and OCS entrants into the Air Force and OCS graduates in the Army. During the period prior to the survey, both the Air Force and Army OCS programs included mostly non-college graduates. These results reveal the high career motivation of such officers and suggest that, if difficulty is experienced with recruiting new college-graduate officers in an all-volunteer environ-

TABLE 6–III.—Expected career retention rate of first-term officers by service and source of commission [1] 1964

Service	Source of Commission					
	All sources	Academy	ROTC [4]	OCS (college graduate)	OCS (non-college graduate) [5]	Direct appointment
Total all services	0.31	0.60	0.26	0.18	0.44	0.16
True volunteers [2]	.46	.65	.42	.24	.62	.31
Draft motivated [3]	.16	.27	.10	.14	.27	.06
Army	.20	.64	.17	—	.48	.12
True volunteer	.38	.68	.31	—	.63	.31
Draft motivated	.13	.41	.06	—	.27	.04
Navy	.25	.59	.18	.15	—	.24
True volunteer	.37	.63	.28	.25	—	.36
Draft motivated	.13	.16	.09	.14	—	.13
Marine Corps	.27	.53	.36	.19	—	.67
True volunteer	.33	.53	.43	.24	—	.67
Draft motivated	.15	—	.21	.13	—	.05
Air Force	.40	.60	.43	—	.44	.15
True volunteer	.56	.67	.55	—	.62	.27
Draft motivated	.21	.26	.19	—	.27	.05

[1] Proportion of officers serving their original obligation who answered "yes" to the question, "Do you intend to remain in service until you are eligible to retire with pay?"

[2] Answered "yes definitely," or "yes probably," to the question of whether they would have entered military service without the draft.

[3] Answered "no definitely" or "no probably" to the question of whether they would have entered military service without the draft.

[4] Includes Navy scholarship holders.

[5] Includes some college graduates in Air Force OCS.

Source: Department of Defense Survey of Active Duty Officers, November 1964.

ment, serious consideration should be given to expanding the non-college officer commissioning programs.

Another interesting aspect of these results is that among the "true volunteers" recruited through the more draft-motivated procurement programs, such as college-graduate OCS, the proportion expecting to make a career in the military was relatively small. This suggests that even with an all-volunteer force and more career-oriented accessions, turnover still will be substantial and a continuous flow of civilian-educated college graduates will enter the force each year.

Although these derived career rates are lower than actual first-term rates, the relative differences between the true volunteer rate and the draft-motivated volunteer rate were used to estimate the increase in officer retention that will accompany a shift to an all-volunteer force.

CHAPTER 7

Recruitment

An expanded and more effective recruiting effort will help supply an all-volunteer force with the desired quality of enlistees. The Commission therefore suggests that the armed services devote an increased proportion of their resources to recruiting and especially to Army recruiting. Studies indicate that a relatively small increase in recruiting expenditures would produce as much as a 10 to 20 percent rise in enlistment rates. Also, modification of existing procedures and increased financial support should yield substantial gains in recruiter productivity.

Since 1961, as shown in table 7-I, the relative proportion of the military's manpower budget devoted to recruiting has remained constant and the number of recruiters has also not increased.

In view of the increased need for enlistments since 1965, the stability of relative recruiting expenditures and the number of recruiters are surprising. They reflect the low priority assigned to recruiting so long as the draft is available to ensure an adequate supply of manpower for the lower ranks. Clearly, elimination of the draft will increase the need for effective recruiting and the budget required. Even if conscription were to continue, the services should devote increased resources to attracting "true" volunteers rather than settling for draftees because the former are more likely to make the military a career.

Obviously, the military benefits more from its investment in an individual who chooses to enlist for three years than from another who is drafted for two. If in-

TABLE 7–I.—Recruiting resources, 1961–69

Fiscal year	Recruiting expenditure as percent of active-duty manpower budget	Total recruiters all services
1961	.0064	7,114
1962	.0056	7,219
1963	.0056	7,070
1964	.0052	6,903
1965	.0057	7,056
1966	.0063	7,241
1967	.0057	7,371
1968	.0054	7,176
1969	.0062	6,987

stead of drafting 33 men who will serve for a total of 66 years (2 years each), the Army can recruit 22 men for a total of 66 years (three years of service each), it will need to train 11 less men over that three-year period. Since one trainer (or supporting person) is required for 11 recruits, enlisting 22 rather than conscripting 33 men will save one trainer. In fiscal 1965, average enlistments per recruiter were roughly 55. A study conducted that year indicated that additional recruiters easily achieved an annual minimum of 22 enlistments and thus "saved" one trainer. Therefore, regardless of whether the draft is maintained, there seems substantial opportunity for the productive addition of more recruiters.

Recruiters play an important role in influencing young men to enlist in the armed services. Ideally, recruiters should be dedicated career men who are skilled in the art of salesmanship. Highly qualified men are in great demand within any institution and the services cannot necessarily have their best men serve as recruiters. Nevertheless, a prospective recruiter should have a positive attitude toward the military as a profession, some aptitude for a public relations role, and a genuine desire to undertake recruiting duty. There is no reason why able recruiters should be automatically rotated to other assignments. Instead, successful recruiters should be allowed to extend their tours of duty, while the unsuccessful are assigned elsewhere.

Every recruiter should receive adequate training before assignment to the field. Such training may be more valuable if it involves greater student participation and less memorization of information and procedures. It would also be desirable for recruiters in the field to share their experience with trainees in school.

Also recommended is an improved incentive system for recruiters. Recognition of successful recruiters could take the form of financial compensation such as extra pay or bonuses as well as accelerated promotions.

We also advocate elimination of the present system under which each district, city, and individual recruiter receives an enlistment quota. Substantial evidence indicates that this system eliminates the incentive to seek enlistees in excess of one's quota.

In addition, the quotas are not always set at appropriate levels. Studies show that cities which do not meet their quotas usually have significantly higher enlistment rates, and that additional recruiters in cities where quotas are met would substantially increase enlistment rates. Elimination of the quota system and institution of more positive incentives should result in higher productivity per recruiter.

In allocating additional resources to recruiting, two- and three-man offices in cities should receive greater priority than one-man offices in smaller communities. Studies have shown that more recruiters at stations in large cities yield greater returns than an equal increase in the number of recruiters in one-man offices in small towns. A greater concentration of recruiting efforts at such stations should be coordinated with more indirect selling and advertising in these larger markets. More advertising in mass media will be both required and rewarding once an all-volunteer force has been instituted, for the elimination of conscription will coincide with improved incentives in the military. Visits to high schools by recruiters, films, performances by special military units, and other appearances will continue to contribute to a positive image for the military.

The British have used such supplementary techniques as the "buddy" system in which enlisted men help persuade their friends to volunteer. This and other new techniques should be tested, especially during the transition to an all-volunteer force.

CHAPTER 8

Conscription of Physicians

The very troublesome problem of conscription of medical doctors has been the subject of independent inquiry by the Commission. Our studies suggest that a variety of steps can be taken to reduce the need for such conscription. Each of these measures will individually contribute something toward eliminating the doctor draft, but we are not certain that they are adequate. Fortunately, given the reduction in forces now planned and the students already committed to military service, there is time not only for further study, but for experimentation with some of the measures suggested, such as increased compensation for military physicians and fellowship programs for medical students.

Eighty percent of all male physicians in the United States under 35 have served in the armed forces or have held reserve commissions. No other group in our society has had such heavy relative demands placed upon it for military service. Only four percent of male physicians under 35 who are eligible for service have not yet served. In the last four years, more than 4,500 doctors entered active-duty service annually—fully 60 percent of the number graduating from medical school each year.

Physicians also suffer the greatest financial loss by having to serve. The pay and allowances received by a young doctor entering military service are approximately one-half the amount he could earn as a civilian. Despite relatively rapid promotions, special pay, continuation pay, etc., a medical officer is significantly underpaid throughout his career. Primarily for this reason, doctors

85

do not usually remain in the military. Sixty percent of all military doctors have served less than two years.

Table 8-I summarizes the size and character of the health service in the armed forces as of January 1, 1969. It encompassed 242 hospitals and 450 reporting dispensaries, and employed over 200,000 people. The patient population slightly exceeded 10,000,000, only 3½ million of whom were active-duty personnel. The other 6½ million were civilians, either dependents of active-duty personnel or retirees or their dependents.

Official accounting for medical services puts the annual budget at $2 billion. Our studies place the expenditures at a considerably higher figure—about $3.25 billion. Moreover, the latter estimates accept military earnings as the cost of both enlisted and officer personnel. If the services of those personnel were priced correctly, that is, at their value in the civilian economy, the cost of military medical service would be even larger. We estimate that the expenditure on medical services rendered by the military medical corps is about $325 per capita as compared to $254 per capita for the entire U.S. population in 1967. The quality of the health care rendered by the military medical corps is generally considered to be very high.

Both the size of the patient population and the personnel requirements in table 8-I reflect the build-up for Vietnam. Those magnitudes will decline with active-duty force reductions.

Table 8-II presents data on the utilization of military medical facilities by type of beneficiary in 1969, and highlights a neglected aspect of conscription. Perhaps one-half of the physicians now conscripted into service are actually serving a civilian population. Despite the increased need for medical services for active-duty personnel as a result of Vietnam, 47 percent of hospital admissions and 48 percent of outpatient visits involved dependents and retired personnel. Presumably, the proportion will be even larger in the post-war environment.

A large centralized health organization has been developed, not just to serve active duty military personnel, but to serve a broad clientele in specialties ranging from obstetrics (146,000 babies delivered in 1969) and pediatrics to geriatrics. Indeed, patient care is only a part of

TABLE 8–I.—Department of Defense medical services

Facilities:	
Hospitals	242
Dispensaries, large reporting	Over 450
Plus laboratories, dental clinics, and other activities	
Manpower:	
Medical Corps	15,972
Dental Corps	6,717
Nurse Corps	11,321
Medical Service Corps	9,397
Biomedical Science Corps	1,043
Army Medical Specialist	613
Veterinary Corps	1,040
Enlisted	109,027
Civil Service *	47,665
Total	202,795
Expenditures (FY 70 estimate) (in millions):	
Health research	$ 104.3
Training and education	132.3
Construction	63.0
Direct hospital and medical services	1,476.8
Indirect hospital and medical services	209.8
Prevention–control of health problems	21.5
Total	$2,007.7
Population eligible for care:	
Active-duty personnel (in millions)	3.40
Dependents of active-duty personnel (in millions)	4.10
Retired, dependents of retired, and dependents of deceased members (in millions)	2.50
Civilians overseas and their dependents (in millions)	.03
Total	10.03

* Includes U.S. and foreign hires, direct and indirect for Army.
Date: Mar. 19, 1969.
Source: Office of the Deputy Assistant Secretary of Defense for Health Affairs.

TABLE 8–II.—Medical care provided at fixed medical facilities in fiscal year 1969

Total number of operating beds	57,477
Beds occupied by active-duty military (daily average)	31,710
Beds occupied by retired uniformed personnel	2,172
Beds occupied by dependents	8,262
Beds occupied by other beneficiaries	1,466
Total number of beds occupied	43,610
Outpatient visits by dependents	23,677,873
Outpatient visits by retired uniformed personnel ..	1,813,575
Total outpatient visits	54,376,229
Admissions of dependents	505,899
Admissions of retired uniformed personnel	59,537
Total admissions	1,272,142
Number of live births	146,145

Source: Office of the Deputy Assistant Secretary of Defense for Health Affairs. Data exclude operations in Southeast Asia.

the organization's activity. It sponsors a variety of medical education and training programs as well as an extensive program of medical research. The desirability of these services is not in question. Good medical care is an attractive inducement to prospective volunteers, and it is one of the more important morale factors for career military personnel. What is in question, however, is whether it is either necessary or advisable to sustain that care with doctors who are compelled to serve.

The professional manpower required to provide these services is drawn from a wide variety of sources but virtually none of the entrants are true volunteers. All but a handful enter because of the threat of being drafted. If the draft is eliminated, dramatic action will be required to insure the continuation of health care now provided by the military medical system.

We have assumed that, whatever steps are taken to convert to a fully voluntary military medical service, the quantity and quality of care supplied to the present patient population will be maintained. Within that constraint there are two courses of action open in converting the system to volunteers. One is to decrease the requirement for military physicians by substituting civilians in their stead. The other is to increase the number of physicians willing to volunteer by improving earnings and other conditions of employment.

Expanded Use of Civilians to Provide Medical Care

A shift of some fraction of military patient care to civilian physicians can be accomplished in either of two ways: (1) by establishing a medical insurance program for some portion of the patient population—the most likely candidates being retirees and their dependents or the dependents of active-duty servicemen, or (2) by engaging civilian physicians to staff some military medical facilities.

A medical insurance scheme is already in effect for retired personnel, and for dependents who can demonstrate that care provided by the military is not available to them. Patients under such a plan obtain medical services from a civilian physician or in a civilian hospital and are reimbursed for the costs. While the substitution of private medical insurance for directly rendered health care is an appealing possibility, it has a number of disadvantages. Shifting patients to the civilian sector would, at least in the near term, further raise costs there. Physicians released from the military could shift to civilian health care, but the hospitals, equipment, etc. could not readily be shifted. To the extent that these military facilities are replaced by a system of private medical insurance, the armed services would reduce their ability to expand available medical care to meet a crisis. Also, substitution of private medical insurance would mean losing the advantages of a unified health care system for the highly mobile population of active-duty dependents.

The substitution of civilian physicians for military doctors within the existing organization could be effected on an individual position basis, but substitution on the scale required is probably possible only through contracting with organized groups of doctors to operate military hospitals or other medical facilities. The present organizational format for most of the health service of the armed forces can best be described as hospital-based group practice.[1] Hospital-based group practice has proved a most efficient form of medical organization in the civilian economy. The Permanente medical groups, for example, provide economical health care for 2 million subscribers in the facilities of the Kaiser Health Foundation. The Defense Department might on a similar basis negotiate contracts with groups of physicians to care for patients in existing military hospitals. Such civilian medical groups would have a number of advantages. They would preserve the hospital-based organizational format, and the advantage of a unified system. They could eliminate duplication of facilities in areas where more than one service maintains health facilities. Where military facilities are underused, the group practice might be expanded to include otherwise ineligible civilians. There would be less turnover of medical personnel and more female doctors. Professional staffing would be easier and less expensive because the physicians would not have to experience many of the disadvantages associated with medical service in the military.

But there are also some disadvantages. With the size of the military medical corps reduced, the number of physicians available for service in a conflict like Vietnam will be smaller. Also, the peacetime rotation of those remaining may be increased and their assignments made less attractive. Conversion of military hospitals to civilian contract operation can proceed only on the basis of careful study of each individual installation. Moreover, care must be taken to preserve desirable assignments for career medical officers and to provide bases for medical education and training. In addition, a careful analysis will be necessary to determine the minimum number of doctors required on active duty by length of service—an analysis based on realistic contingency plans and on rotation base requirements for planned force levels.

Increasing the Number of Physicians Who Volunteer

Physicians, like other active-duty personnel, make career decisions on the basis of a wide variety of pecuniary and

---

[1] The remainder consists of large and small medical units in direct support of combat units.

non-pecuniary aspects of the careers under consideration. These include potential earnings, available facilities and equipment, security, prestige, opportunities for further education and research, type of patient, patient/physician relationships, etc. The attractiveness of military medical careers can no doubt be enhanced by improving some of the non-pecuniary factors. However, the gap between civilian and military medical income is now so large, and the number of true volunteers is so small, that such improvements do not touch the heart of the problem. Something substantial must be done about pecuniary rewards for military physicians to obtain a voluntary military medical corps. There are again two major alternatives. One is to provide stipends to medical students in exchange for a commitment to serve for a specified period. The other is to raise the pay of medical officers.[2] The extent to which reliance is placed on one or the other of these two depends upon the size career medical force it is desirable to maintain. Stipends for medical students will provide a broad base of young physicians, most of whom will not elect careers in the military. Increasing the pay for medical officers, on the other hand, will significantly effect retention. Indeed, the compensation schedule for physicians should be designed specifically to provide efficiently the desired number and length of service distribution of doctors. In this regard, the military's retirement system is inefficient within the context of the medical corps because it permits military physicians to retire with full benefits (about half salary) after 20 years of service and embark on a civilian career. After twenty years, these doctors are relatively young and still capable of serving effectively.

A variety of forms of subsidies to medical students are feasible. Differences between civilian and military earnings for doctors suggest that a stipend of $5,000 per year paid to medical students over seven years (four years of medical school, one year of internship, and two years of residency) would produce a significant flow of volunteers willing to commit themselves to three years of active

[2] Another possibility, the establishment of a military medical college, has been proposed a number of times in the past. While this may be desirable, the number of doctors such a college would produce is very small relative to the number required and the first graduates probably would not be available for a decade.

duty. Variations on this basic arrangement could include larger stipends for shorter periods or smaller stipends for shorter service commitments. Such stipends could be tied into already existing plans for bringing medical students into the military.

Data to use as a basis for reliable estimates of the effect of compensation on the number of physicians who would

TABLE 8–III.—Proposed compensation for medical officers

Active service	Officer rank	Annual salary [1]	Physician continuation pay [2]	Physician pay	Medical officer total salary
Over					
1	O-3	$11,034	0	$ 1,800	$12,834
2	O-3	11,456	0	1,800	13,256
3	O-3	11,456	0	3,600	15,056
4	O-3	11,794	0	5,400	17,194
5	O-4	12,320	0	7,200	19,520
6	O-4	13,000	0	9,000	22,000
7	O-4	13,000	0	10,800	23,800
8	O-4	13,601	0	12,600	26,201
9	O-4	13,601	$2,822	12,600	29,023
10	O-4	14,116	2,950	12,600	29,666
11	O-5	14,953	3,120	12,600	30,673
12	O-5	15,889	3,356	12,600	31,845
13	O-5	15,889	3,356	12,600	31,845
14	O-5	16,659	3,549	12,600	32,808
15	O-5	16,659	3,549	12,600	32,808
16	O-5	17,084	3,655	12,600	33,339
17	O-6	18,780	4,041	12,600	35,421
18	O-6	19,719	4,276	12,600	36,595
19	O-6	19,719	4,276	12,600	36,595
20	O-6	19,719	5,701	12,600	38,020
21	O-6	19,719	5,701	12,600	38,020
22	O-6	21,170	6,185	12,600	39,955

[1] This is as of July 1, 1969, and includes basic pay plus basic allowance for quarters and basic allowance for subsistence. Total compensation would be higher due to various special pays and retirement benefits. Special pays can be used to reward doctors for advanced certification.

[2] Continuation pay is already in effect.

enter the military or the number who would remain
there are not available. For that reason, a provisional
approach to medical pay seems advisable. Data on civilian earnings for medical doctors are available, and have
been used to develop the compensation profiles shown in
table 8-III. Columns 3 and 4 of table 8-III give the annual salary and continuation pay for medical officers as
of July 1, 1969. At present medical officers with 2–6 years
of active duty also receive an additional $150 a month
as special physician pay. Column 5 sets forth a new
schedule of physician pay as follows:

Third year of duty	$300 a month
Fourth year of duty	$450 a month
Fifth year of duty	$600 a month
Sixth year of duty	$750 a month
Seventh year of duty	$900 a month
Eighth year of duty	$1,050 a month

The last column of table 8-III gives the sum of these
three components of compensation. The total salaries
shown in column 6 compare reasonably well with those
of physicians in group practice, except in the early years
where they are lower to take account of the student
stipends discussed above. If student support is not undertaken, or if individuals wish to join the military who
have not participated in the fellowship program, the
total salary in the early years would have to be adjusted
upward.

We believe that the salary schedule derived in table
8-III is a major step toward a fully voluntary medical
corps, and recommend that it be put into effect at the
same time as the recommended pay increase for the rest
of the force, July 1, 1970.

Transition to a Voluntary Medical Corps

The transition to a voluntary medical corps will be
greatly facilitated by planned reductions in force levels.
As a result of draft pressure, many medical students have
already committed themselves to service under the various
programs now in effect. With those already committed
and with prompt action on stipends for graduate students

and increased pay for military physicians, it should be possible to eliminate the conscription of doctors concurrently with the ending of the draft for other military personnel.

Because of uncertainties over the extent to which substitution of civilians will be possible, our estimates of the budget increase required to move to a voluntary medical service are imprecise. Given the recommended pay increase, the fellowship program, and the cost of civilian staffed hospitals, we estimate that an additional $150 million to $200 million of expenditures will be required.[3]

[3] While this chapter has addressed only the question of achieving an all-volunteer force of physicians, the procurement and retention of professionals for the military in other health disciplines pose similar, though somewhat less severe, problems which must also be addressed.

CHAPTER 9

Reserves

Introduction

The Commission recognized from its first meeting the need for special attention to the problem of the reserve forces. Surveys indicate that perhaps 75 percent of the enlisted personnel fulfilling their initial six-year military service obligation in the reserves are there only because of the draft. If conscription is eliminated, how are these forces to be manned? Research directed to that question indicates that planned reserves can be maintained on an all-volunteer basis at reasonable levels of compensation. Analysis of the reserve problem, however, suffers seriously from a lack of data. Even though special care was taken to provide against errors of estimation, the assessments of what is required to maintain an all-volunteer reserve force are much more tenuous than those for the active-duty force.

United States reserve forces have two primary functions: first, to supplement the active-duty forces as needed; second, to help maintain domestic peace and assist in time of civil disaster. The latter is largely the responsibility of the National Guard.

Currently, about one million officers and men in the Ready Reserve receive pay for participating in reserve training—two-thirds of them are in the Army Reserve (USAR) and Army National Guard. More than 80 percent of the men in the paid reserve are organized and trained as units which are designed to fit into the structure of the active forces. Should these men be called to active duty, it is intended that they perform in their respective units. The remaining 20 percent, about 165,000 men, can be called as individuals to augment active forces. In addition to paid reservists, there are 1.3 million unpaid reservists in the Ready Reserve pool who may be called up as individuals.

Discussion

In an emergency the President is authorized to call to active duty as many as one million Ready Reservists (10 USC 673). Reserves in the Standby and Retired categories can be called only with the approval of Congress. Table 9-I shows how reserve manpower (less mobilized strength still on active duty) was allocated into recall categories on June 30, 1969. Table 9-II summarizes the major units which that strength provided in FY 1969.

Reserve Force Requirements

The impact of planned reductions in active-duty forces on reserve force manning requirements is still very uncertain. Four projected active-duty forces have been analyzed, spanning the range that is generally considered reasonable, from 2.0 million to 3.0 million men. A similar procedure has been followed in analyzing the reserves. We have associated a reserve force, by service, with each of the four active alternatives. The projected strengths shown in columns 3 and 4 of table 9-III are based on the relationship between active and reserve forces prior to Vietnam.[1]

There is reason to doubt, however, that there was a real requirement for the pre-Vietnam levels of paid-drill strength. The public record is clear that the Army was reluctant to accept the minimum strength levels mandated by Congress. The Air Force was similarly pressured into higher levels than it had requested, although the Air Force found useful work for much of the excess strength, largely

[1] The reserve analysis omits the Navy's "2 x 6" program from strength and enlistment calculations. It is included in the analysis of the active forces. Its strength ranges from 18,000 at the 2 million level to 24,000 at the 3 million level.

TABLE 9–I.—Defense Department reserve forces *
June 30, 1969
[thousands]

Paid drill Ready Reserve	Officers	Enlisted	Total
Army National Guard	30.4	358.5	389.0
Army Reserve	32.2	229.1	261.3
Naval Reserve	19.0	113.7	132.7
Marine Corps Reserve	2.7	46.4	49.1
Air National Guard	10.3	73.1	83.4
Air Force Reserve	10.1	34.9	44.9
Total DOD	104.7	855.7	960.4
Other paid Ready Reserve	19.3	37.7	57.0
Total paid status	124.0	893.4	1,017.4
Unpaid Ready Reserve	98.3	1,189.0	1,287.3
Standby Reserve	103.7	322.2	425.9
Retired Reserve	323.8	205.0	528.8
Total not on active duty ...	649.8	2,609.6	3,259.4

* The U.S. Coast Guard Reserve is administered in peacetime by the Secretary of Transportation with the concurrence of the Secretary of the Navy. On June 30, 1969, it included 17,800 Selected Reserve (paid drill) and 9,800 reinforcements. Because of time limitations, we have not specifically considered Coast Guard problems.

TABLE 9–II.—Major reserve units
June 30, 1969

Army Reserve	Naval Reserve	Air Force Reserve
13 training divisions	35 destroyers and destroyer escorts	14 wings (45 squadrons)
3 brigades	28 boats and craft	8 military airlift
2 maneuver area commands	36 air squadrons	6 tactical airlift

Army Guard	Marine Reserve	Air Guard
8 divisions	1 division	21 wings (92 squadrons)
18 brigades	1 air wing	12 fighter
		3 reconnaissance
		2 air refueling
		7 military airlift

TABLE 9–III.—Alternative active and reserve strength levels [thousands]

Active duty		Reserves			
		Unmodified enlisted strength [1]		Modified enlisted strength [1]	
(1)					
Total force level	(2) Enlisted strength	(3) Mixed force	(4) Volunteer force [2]	(5) Mixed force	(6) Volunteer force [2]
2,000	1,697.1	628.3	639.5	554.9	568.5
2,250	1,902.7	707.5	712.4	624.8	632.3
2,500	2,107.8	786.0	785.5	694.1	696.3
3,000	2,581.1	838.8	829.8	740.9	734.9

[1] Excludes the "2x6" program in the Naval Reserve.

[2] The alternative reserve requirements estimates shown use the concept of equal effectiveness discussed in chapter 4. Like the active forces, the reserves will experience savings accruing from reduced personnel turnover. However, not much reduction in turnover will result from lengthened first enlistments which are now predominantly for 6 years. The principal source of reduced turnover will be higher re-enlistment rates in the first 6 to 10 years of service. The effect on reserve manning requirements is attenuated, however, because most reserve trainees receive their initial training from the active establishment.

In addition, the reduction in turnover from higher retention is offset by a decline in the number of prior-service reserve enlistments owing to lower turnover in a voluntary active force. Recruits from civilian life must make up the shortfall, and they enlarge the share of noneffectives in the force. The net result is that the higher proportion of civilian enlistments outweighs the gain from higher retention at levels up to about 2.5 million.

in part-time support of the active force's mission. The tenuous nature of the pre-Vietnam reserve requirements is also evident from independent research undertaken by the Commission staff, which confirms that reorganization of the reserve forces could eliminate approximately 113,000 men in paid drill status ("spaces") without significantly affecting reserve effectiveness.

Because of these apparent overstrengths, we have prepared a second set of alternative reserve force levels to be associated with the four alternative active levels. This second set modifies the first by removing from the current level 110,000 Army and 2,800 Air Force paid-drill spaces (16,300 officer and 96,500 enlisted spaces). Proportional modifications are made in each representative force level and are presented as "modified" levels in table 9-III.

These force levels are set forth here to emphasize that shortfalls from present levels in the reserves are *not* a serious threat to national security. We believe that the recommended pay increase for the active-duty component (which is automatically effective for the reserves) will provide enough reserve enlistments to meet the larger requirements in table 9-III. If that turns out not to be true, or if transitional problems develop, reserve strength could decline moderately from the unmodified levels in table 9-III without posing a serious national security problem.

Reserve Non-Prior Service Accessions

The critical variable in determining the feasibility of a voluntary reserve force is the number of enlistments from civilian life that will be required annually. That number depends on: (1) annual reserve losses (which depend on the reserve re-enlistment rate), and (2) annual prior service enlistments (those who join the reserves after active duty). Columns 3 and 5 of table 9-IV show estimates of the number of civilian enlistments required annually to maintain each of the forces shown in columns 2 and 4 on a stable basis.

TABLE 9–IV.—Annual civilian enlistments required for volunteer reserve alternatives [1]
[thousands]

Active force level	Unmodified enlisted strength [1]	Civilian enlistments required	Modified enlisted strength [1]	Civilian enlistments required
2,000	639.5	90.0	568.5	76.2
2,250	712.4	97.2	632.3	81.6
2,500	785.5	106.2	696.3	88.6
3,000	829.8	102.6	734.9	84.0

[1] Re-enlistments are estimated to be 13 percent of force strength; prior service enlistments vary with active losses. The derivation of these estimates is described below.

For comparison, the annual number of civilian enlistments in the reserves (excluding the "2 x 6" program)
averaged 122,000 during the last eight years.

The Supply of Reserve Manpower

Like the active forces, the paid drill reserve contains
a mixture of true volunteers and men who serve chiefly
or solely to discharge the military service obligation
imposed by law. The proportion of men who willingly
undertake regular drill training is strikingly different for
officers than for enlisted men. According to a 1969 Defense Department survey of reserve personnel, 80 percent
of officers drill voluntarily, but only 27 percent of enlisted
men. For this reason, our analysis has focused on the
enlisted segment of an all-volunteer reserve force.

The prospect of securing volunteers for reserve service is surely related to pay levels. All too often it is
said that drill pay is nearly irrelevant to a young man
deciding whether to devote free time to unit activity. Yet
almost one-third of men with less than six years of service describe drill pay as one of the most significant
factors in their decision.

A typical reservist attends 48 training assemblies per
year. Each assembly lasts four hours (a small percentage
only three) and assemblies are usually "multiple": two
on Saturday, or four on a weekend. On average, the
typical reservist devotes one full weekend each month to
unit training and trains for two weeks on active duty each
year. His total investment of time is 312 hours. Count-
ing basic pay alone, he earns $642 a year if he is an E4
(corporal) with four years of service (about $580 if he
has three years of service).

This is not a large amount compared to total family
earnings: median income for an E4 falls in the $7,000-
$8,000 range. But the more meaningful economic com-
parison is with part-time employment alternatives. Two-
thirds of the E4's are married and more than half of them
have working wives. Two-thirds of the E4's are 21-25
years old; and more than one-third have children. The
typical E4, in other words, closely resembles the Department of Labor's portrait of the typical multiple job holder—

"a comparatively young married man with children who feels a financial squeeze." According to the Bureau of Labor Statistics, in May 1966, 5½ percent of 20–24-year-old working men held multiple jobs. They worked a median 14 hours on their second job. In a full 52-week year, they would work 728 extra hours.

For men who are interested in extra income, reserve activity does not offer the earnings potential of part-time civilian work because it is too infrequent. For some men it could become an attractive alternative as a second job. Certainly a necessary if not sufficient condition for voluntary reserve participation is a level of drill pay attractive enough to make military instruction preferable to other part-time activities. While the pay level in the early years of service has been too low to attract voluntarily the high quality of recruits which the reserves have enjoyed over the past ten years, our studies show that a more reasonable qualitative mix can be obtained voluntarily.

Drill pay is now directly linked to active-duty basic pay. The present pay schedule is given in table 9-VI. In one drill period (usually four hours), a reservist earns an amount equal to a full day's pay for his regular service counterpart. His starting level, if he enlists directly from civilian life, is about $1.00 per hour. (The federal minimum wage is $1.60 per hour.) A man who has served four years with the regular forces and has reached the E5 (sergeant) pay grade can earn $2.75 per hour at drill training. At the career end of the scale, the rates are quite attractive. A First Sergeant with over 16 years of service earns $5.00 per hour.[2]

Our pay recommendations will increase these hourly rates significantly in the lower grades. In his first year of service, a recruit will earn $2.00-$2.50 per hour, approaching the pay that a sergeant now receives. Drill pay will be increased above the amount needed to maintain its present relation to civilian wages as shown in table 9-V.

In addition to basic pay, certain special and incentive compensation, such as flying pay and parachute pay, is

[2] Costs of travel to and from drill assemblies are borne by the individual.

TABLE 9–V.—Drill-pay increase by length of service

Years of service	Percent
0–1	89.8
1–2	64.4
2–3	23.7
3–4	19.5
4–5	8.3
5–6	7.9
6–7	4.9
7–8	7.2
8–10	5.0

paid to those on inactive duty at the daily active rate. While on active duty, the reservist receives the same pay as the regular. Occupational differentials, such as proficiency pay and the variable re-enlistment bonus, are not paid to reservists on either active or inactive duty.

Reservists are also entitled to pensions. Full retirement credit is given for years served on active duty; partial credit is given for years on inactive service. Retired pay is contingent upon completion of twenty creditable years of service and begins at age 60, at the pay scale then in effect.

Proposals are advanced from time to time to permit payment of retired pay at age 50. If this were done and benefits were not reduced, the cost of the retirement benefit would double. Since retirement pay has little attraction for young men whose primary job is in the civilian sector, this added expenditure would do little to solve the recruitment problems of the reserves.

Currently, about 850,000 enlisted men are in paid-drill reserve status. If men temporarily called to active duty are included, the paid-drill total averaged 836,000 over the eight years prior to June, 1969. To maintain this level the reserves have required an average annual inflow of 262,000 men. Of these, 153,000—nearly 60 percent—were men who entered directly from civil life.[3] The remaining 109,000 were personnel with prior service.

[3] Includes over 35,000 in the Navy's "2 x 6" program.

TABLE 9–VI.—Pay rates per training assembly (dollars)
[effective July 1, 1969]

Pay grade						Years in pay grade								
	Under 2	Over 2	Over 3	Over 4	Over 6	Over 8	Over 10	Over 12	Over 14	Over 16	Over 18	Over 20	Over 22	Over 26
O10														
O9														
O8	48.44	49.89	51.07	51.07	51.07	54.88	54.88	57.47	57.47	59.85	62.47	64.85	67.46	67.46
O7	40.24	42.99	42.99	42.99	44.90	44.90	47.50	47.50	49.89	54.88	58.66	58.66	58.66	58.66
O6	29.81	32.77	34.91	34.91	34.91	34.91	34.91	34.91	36.11	41.80	43.94	44.90	47.50	51.53
O5	23.84	28.02	29.94	29.94	29.94	29.94	30.87	32.51	34.69	35.04	39.43	40.61	42.04	
O4	20.12	24.47	26.13	26.13	26.59	27.78	29.68	31.34	31.42	34.20	35.16			
O3	18.70	20.89	22.31	24.71	25.88	26.83	28.27	29.68	30.40					
O2	14.98	17.80	21.38	22.09	22.55									
O1	12.88	14.25	17.80											
O3 *				24.71	25.88	26.83	28.27	29.68	30.87					
O2 *				22.09	22.55	23.27	24.47	25.42	26.13					
O1 *				17.80	19.00	19.71	20.42	21.13	22.09					
W4	19.04	20.42	20.42	20.89	21.84	22.80	23.74	25.42	26.55	27.55	28.27	29.20	30.17	32.51

Footnotes are found at the end of the table.

TABLE 9–VI.—Pay rates per training assembly (dollars).—Continued
[effective July 1, 1969]

Pay grade	Under 2	Over 2	Over 3	Over 4	Over 6	Over 8	Over 10	Over 12	Over 14	Over 16	Over 18	Over 20	Over 22	Over 26
W3	17.30	18.78	18.78	19.00	19.24	20.55	21.84	22.55	23.27	23.97	24.71	25.66	26.59	27.55
W2	15.15	16.39	16.39	16.86	17.80	18.78	19.49	20.18	20.80	21.61	22.31	23.02	23.97	
W1	12.63	14.49	14.49	15.68	16.39	17.10	17.80	18.53	19.24	19.95	20.65	21.38		
E9							21.63	22.12	22.64	23.13	23.64	24.11	25.39	27.85
E8						18.15	18.65	19.15	19.65	20.15	20.63	21.14	22.39	24.88
E7	11.40	13.66	14.17	14.68	15.17	15.66	16.15	16.67	17.41	17.91	18.41	18.65	19.90	22.39
E6	9.82	11.93	12.43	12.93	13.44	13.92	14.43	15.17	15.66	16.15	16.41			
E5	8.49	10.46	10.95	11.44	12.19	12.69	13.18	13.66	13.92					
E4	7.13	8.95	9.44	10.19	10.69									
E3	5.16	7.20	7.71	8.20										
E2	4.25	5.96												
E1	4.10	5.46												
E1 < 4 mos.	3.83													

* Commissioned officers in the grade of O1 through O3 credited with over 4 years' active enlisted service.

Three sources of manpower are available to an all-volunteer paid drill reserve:

1. Re-enlistments—new commitments by those already in the reserves. Re-enlistments affect losses and thereby the level of accessions required to maintain a given force;
2. Prior service enlistments—enlistments by those who have been on active duty; and
3. Civilian enlistments—first enlistments by civilians.

Re-Enlistments

Reserve re-enlistments are a primary factor in determining the number of new accessions required each year. Re-enlistment rates may be expressed as a proportion of average strength. Measured in this way, re-enlistment rates during the FY 1962-69 period are shown in table 9-VII.

These data imply that if the re-enlistment propensities of the FY 1962-65 period could be re-established, a 20 percent improvement (from 7.2 percent to 8.6 percent) in re-enlistments would result. Since FY 1962 and 1963 were very poor years owing to the crises in Berlin and

TABLE 9–VII.—Paid-drill strength, re-enlistments, and re-enlistment rates
FY 1962–69 [thousands]

FY	Strength	Re-enlistments	Rate (percent)
1962	851.6	54.3	6.4
1963	820.3	59.5	7.3
1964	799.7	88.3	11.0
1965	818.7	81.1	9.9
1966	833.5	*80.9	9.7
1967	863.2	*68.4	7.9
1968	856.4	*51.5	6.0
1969	856.7	*43.3	5.1
1962-65.........	3,290.3	283.2	8.6
1966-69.........	3,409.8	244.1	7.2

* Includes estimated 1.9 for Marine Corps.

Cuba and subsequent reorganizations of the Army reserve components, the improvement might well be greater.

The conventional and more useful way of analyzing re-enlistment rates is to examine the proportions of separating men who continue in service at a series of "decision points" along the career path. Because actual rates are not available, we used statements of continuation intentions provided by the 1969 attitude survey to approximate them. Table 9-VIII displays re-enlistment intentions classified by length of service and by obligated and voluntary drill categories. As one would expect, interest in drill

TABLE 9–VIII.—Men in 48 drill programs stating firm intention to continue paid-drill participation, 1969

Years of service	Required to drill (percent)	Voluntary drill (percent)
Less than 6........	3.4	12.4
3–4	3.0	8.2
5–6	4.3	13.5
6–10	19.2	50.7
6–8	15.5	46.9
8–10	52.2	57.6

participation is higher in the voluntary category; and it is markedly higher after the sixth year of service.

What would have been the effect on re-enlistments if the 1969 reserves had been composed entirely of volunteers? Using re-enlistment intentions as proxies for re-enlistment rates, we have estimated that "conversion" to a volunteer force would have added nearly 33,000 re-enlistments, an increase of three-fourths over the number who actually did re-enlist in FY 1969. The re-enlistment rate, expressed as a percentage of average strength, would have improved from 5.1 to 8.8 percent. (About half of this estimated gain occurred in the under-6-year portion of the force, where the conventional re-enlistment rate— percent of men separating—rose from 6 percent, in the mixed force, to 16 percent in the all-volunteer force.)

This comparison suggests that a shift to voluntarism would raise the 7.2 percent re-enlistment rate of recent years to 12.7 percent of average strength. The best re-enlistment experience in the eight years examined was FY 1964, when 88,000 re-enlistments equaled 11 percent of a mixed volunteer/obligated force. Given the striking differences in re-enlistment attitudes between volunteers and non-volunteers, the estimate that a voluntary force will attain re-enlistments at that level seems quite conservative.

One might assume an additional increase resulting from re-establishment of the pre-1965 environment. If this were the case, the re-enlistment rate would become 15.2 percent of average strength. We did not make that assumption; because the earlier force included a larger proportion of volunteers and the shift to voluntarism was, thus, already partly taken into account.

We then estimated the effect which our proposed pay increases would have on re-enlistment behavior. Survey responses indicate that modest increases in re-enlistment will occur. Higher pay will induce proportionately more re-enlistments among men who now have the lowest inclination to continue in reserve service. For instance, our studies show that among those persons required to drill with from four to six years of service, a pay increase of 10 percent would be likely to increase the re-enlistment rate from 3.6 to 4.3 percent, an increase of 20 percent. Re-enlistment rates for those who drill voluntarily would rise from 15.2 to 16.4 percent, only an 8 percent improvement. Volunteers with six to ten years of service now tend to re-enlist at very high rates—50.7 percent according to survey statements. A 10 percent increase in their pay would raise their re-enlistment rate to 52.3 percent, a 3 percent improvement.

We propose to increase enlisted drill pay 6 percent after the sixth year of service, when most decisions to continue in the reserves are made. This increase will have both immediate and longer-term effects on re-enlistments. The immediate result will be to provide a moderate rise in re-enlistments of those in the first six years of service. Such men now usually leave the reserves, but they are more responsive to pay changes than their older colleagues. As volunteer enlistees gradually replace draft-motivated men over the six years following conversion to an all-volunteer force, re-enlistment rates will improve at accelerating rates until a higher stable rate is reached. Our calculations indicate that, in an "all-volunteer" 1969 reserve, re-enlistments as a percent of strength would have risen from 8.8 percent (after conversion) to 9.1 percent (after the pay rise); and half of this gain would be realized in the under-six-year component of the force.

The recommended pay increase should improve the position of reserve drill duty vis-a-vis other part-time employment opportunities. If relative pay is maintained at the recommended level in an all-volunteer situation, we estimate that the combined effect of moving to a volunteer system and increasing pay will increase the re-enlistment rate from the current 7.2 percent to 13 percent, an improvement of 80 percent.

Prior Service Enlistments

The man who separates from active service is a highly prized candidate for service in a reserve unit. He has had two or more years of training and experience which qualify him not only for immediate assignment to fill a unit vacancy, but often for a leadership role as well. Under present rules, geography prevents full exploitation of this enlistment potential. Unless a unit with a vacancy matching his grade and skill qualification is convenient to his home and regular occupation, a veteran is unable to participate. Because unit assignment specifies location many prior-service enlistments have been lost.

In the eight years spanning FY 1962-69, 4.8 million men left active service. The reserve components recruited fewer than 900,000 of them into paid drill status. That total includes substantial numbers who were obligated to join, some through training "pay-back" agreements entered into during their active service, but more through involuntary assignment (in the Army Reserve) to achieve programmed strength levels. The number of enlistments would have been still smaller had not the Navy assigned a large fraction of reservists to paid-drill, individual mobilization billets rather than to actual crews. Nearly 80 percent of paid-drill Naval reservists attend regular training sessions during the year and report to a crew assignment for two-week summer training. The Navy's experience demonstrates that it is not necessary to forfeit reserve enlistments because of the self-imposed limitations of unit structure.

Prior-service recruitment experience between FY 1962 and 1969 deteriorated sharply except in the Navy, where the "2x6" program provided a degree of stability. The drop was sharpest in the Army components, especially the USAR, whose recruitment rate fell from nearly 23 percent in the first four years to 6 percent in the last four. This decline is attributable chiefly to wartime and the accompanying sharp rise in the number of inductees separated: 70 percent of 1960-67 inductions were released in the 1966-69 period. Another factor depressing USAR recruitment was a ruling by the Defense Department in June 1967 that involuntary assignments into paid-drill units were to be used only if programmed strength could not otherwise be attained.

Since the 1962-65 period approximates a non-war recruiting situation, we have chosen that period as the basis for estimates of enlistments in a post-Vietnam environment. As a matter of policy, the reserves accepted prior-service men only on a voluntary basis during that period, except the USAR. Even so, survey responses in 1964 show that fractions of the men in the other components also regarded their service as involuntary. These responses may be only the results of retrospection, but they suggest that estimates of potential recruits ought to be discounted for involuntary assignment in all components. The adjusted rate is the number of enlistments multiplied by the fraction who volunteered, the product then divided by the number of separations from the parent service. Table 9-IX presents the unadjusted and voluntary (or adjusted) rates which we applied to projected active separations in order to estimate reserve gains from that source. The high level of voluntarism in the National Guard, and to somewhat lesser degree in the Navy, is striking.

Projected losses from the 2.5 million all-volunteer force are 342,300 in the 1977-79 period which would provide 47,800 prior service enlistments for the reserves. Projected losses from the 2.25 million all-volunteer force of the 1977-79 period are 302,500. We estimate that the reserves will be able to recruit about 42,400 of them.

**TABLE 9–IX.—Percent of active separations enlisting
in reserve components
[FY 1962–65]**

Reserve component	Percent of active loss into paid drill	Voluntary proportion	Voluntary enlistment rate
Army National Guard .	8.5	.944	8.0
Army Reserve	22.8	.257	5.9
Naval Reserve	31.5	.811	25.5
Marine Corps Reserve .	10.1	.404	4.1
Air National Guard	4.7	.943	4.4
Air Force Reserve	6.0	.601	3.6

Substantially higher gains can be expected during the early years of transition to an all-volunteer force owing to high separations from the active force. For instance, active separations from a 1971 all-volunteer force are predicted to be 665,000. We estimate that the reserves could voluntarily enlist 92,000, or nearly double the number expected after the active force is stabilized at 2.5 million. Table 9-X consolidates active separations and projected gains into the reserves.

Civilian Enlistments

In the presence of the draft, reserve service has provided an attractive opportunity for young men to minimize the personal cost of fulfilling their military obligation. Indeed, it has come to be preferred by so many that queues of prospective enlistees have formed which at times are longer than the entire annual flow of enlistments. The reserves, unable to accept all applicants, have exercised a high degree of selectivity. Table 9-XI compares the educational attainment of reserve and active-duty personnel. In 1969, 94 percent of the paid-drill reservists had completed high school, over one-half had attended college, and 16 percent had been granted college degrees. This is a much higher level of educational attainment than for the active-duty force. Only 1.6 percent of paid-drill reservists were Negro, as compared to 10.5

TABLE 9-X.—Projected active separations and paid drill gains, all-volunteer active and reserve forces, selected years
[thousands]

Component	Rate (percent)	1971 Sep.	1971 Gains	1972 Sep.	1972 Gains	1973 Sep.	1973 Gains	Average 1977–79 Sep.	Average 1977–79 Gains
2.5 million active force									
Army National Guard	8.0	} 406	32.5	} 322	25.8	} 296	23.7	} 148	11.9
Army Reserve	5.9		23.9		19.0		17.5		8.7
Naval Reserve	25.5	99	25.3	103	26.4	111	28.4	75	19.0
Marine Corps Reserve	4.1	71	2.9	69	2.8	42	1.7	34	1.4
Air National Guard	4.4	} 89	3.9	} 99	4.3	} 102	4.5	} 85	3.8
Air Force Reserve	3.6		3.2		3.6		3.7		3.1
Total		665	91.7	593	81.8	551	79.5	342	47.8
2.25 million active force									
Army National Guard	8.0	} 406	32.5	} 322	25.8	} 296	23.7	} 121	9.7
Army Reserve	5.9		23.9		19.0		17.5		7.2
Naval Reserve	25.5	99	25.3	103	26.4	110	28.0	70	17.9
Marine Corps Reserve	4.1	71	2.9	69	2.8	42	1.7	33	1.3
Air National Guard	4.4	} 89	3.9	} 99	4.3	} 102	4.5	} 78	3.4
Air Force Reserve	3.6		3.2		3.6		3.7		2.8
Total		665	91.7	593	81.8	550	79.1	303	42.4

percent in the active forces. At the same time fewer than
5 percent of paid drill reservists, but 15 percent of active-
duty enlisted men, were under the age of twenty. Table
9-XII compares reserve and active distribution by age.

TABLE 9–XI.—**Educational attainment of enlisted men—
FY 1969**
[cumulative percent]

	Paid drill reserves	Active duty
College graduates	16.1	2.2
Some college	54.4	21.5
High school graduates.	93.9	82.7

TABLE 9–XII.—**Age of enlisted men—FY 1969**
[cumulative percent]

	Paid drill reserves	Active duty
Under 19	1.2	5.6
Under 20	4.8	15.2
Under 22	19.1	47.8
Under 24	40.9	66.9
Under 26	62.2	75.0

Men of this age and educational level are almost certain to have little real interest in reserve service. The
1969 survey found that three-fourths of the paid-drill
reservists serving their initial six-year obligation entered
military service because of the draft. Five years earlier
the proportion was two-thirds. (Among 17–21-year-olds
in the 1969 survey, the proportion was 55 percent.)

Evidence of strong draft motivation among reservists
has been interpreted to mean that a voluntary system will
not work. These draft motivation data, however, significantly overstate the magnitude of the problem. As table
9-XIII shows, draft motivation is strongly related to education and age: the younger and less educated the reservist
the lower the draft motivation. If recruitment is focused
on a younger, less well educated group the flow of volunteers will be substantially larger than is implied by the
draft motivation of the present force.

In estimating the number of civilian men who can be

TABLE 9–XIII.—Percent draft motivated by education attained and by age, fiscal years 1964 and 1969

Educational attainment	1964	1969
College graduate	90	91
2–4 years' college	77	83
Under 2 years' college	60	73
High school graduate	43	70
Less than high school graduate ..	24	64

Age		
21	83	85
20	70	76
19	55	78
18	41	65
Under 18	26	54

recruited for reserve service, we have noted the large waiting lists for reserve vacancies. These lists were built up because the ability of the services to accept reserve enlistments has been limited by their budgets and by the capability of the active forces to provide initial training. At the same time, the services' needs for new enlistments are governed by losses which follow a complex cyclical pattern, with crises such as Berlin influencing losses in later years. The size of the queues has fluctuated as capacity and needs varied, and it has not been possible to estimate satisfactorily the additional number of volunteers who might have been recruited if enlistments had been unlimited. Table 9-XIV shows the size of waiting lists annually since 1965 (the first year for which data are available) and the number of enlistments which occurred in the corresponding fiscal year.

While our estimates do not use data on the queue explicitly, we have used the existence of the queues to justify basing our estimates on recruitment in a high pre-war year—1964.

As shown above, educational attainments and mental qualifications have been inflated in the reserves under the pressure of the draft. The reserves do not require such an

**TABLE 9–XIV.—Numbers of men awaiting reserve
enlistment on January 1st and numbers enlisted,
FY 1965–69
[thousands]**

	1965	1966	1967	1968	1969	1970
Waiting	236.9	153.2	272.2	125.2	81.9	148.2
Enlisted (REP)* .	117.9	204.7	96.3	61.9	112.7	xx

* Reserve Enlisted Programs.

educationally rich force. Peacetime recruits should come predominantly from among high school graduates and not from those with some college experience. According to the 1964 survey: 43 percent of the high school graduates in their first term of reserve service were draft-motivated enlistees; 55 percent of those 17-21 in the first term were draft motivated; 67 percent of those 17-24 were draft motivated; and 70 percent of the last-named group, excluding the "2 x 6" program, were draft-motivated. Even though that group contained far more college men than is desirable for good retention, we have used a draft motivation factor of 70 percent in projecting enlistments. In 1964, 175,000 men enlisted from civil life. If 30 percent were true volunteers, the true volunteers represented 0.7 percent of the 17–21-year-old pool. For our projections we have assumed that at current levels of relative military/civilian pay, civilian reserve enlistments each year would be 0.7 percent of the 17–21-year pool. Our estimates take no account of the fact that entry-level drill pay rose substantially more than earnings of civilian production workers in the five years following 1964, and therefore err on the conservative side.

We have no data from which to estimate the effects of pay increases on reserve enlistments. Our analyses of the problem of recruiting into the active forces indicate that a pay increase of one percent will produce a 1.25 percent increase in enlistment rates; our estimates of reserve re-enlistments suggest that a one percent pay increase will generate only 0.8 percent improvement in re-enlistments. Table 9-XV portrays projected enlistments under each of these assumptions and at an intermediate value.

Summary

Table 9-XVI shows required reserve force strengths and enlistments for stable forces corresponding to the 2.25 and 2.5 million man active forces. Table 9-XVI also shows three projections of voluntary enlistments for the reserve forces. The projected enlistments appear to be adequate for the reserve forces associated with the 2.25 million force and 2.5 million man active forces. Given the uncertainty which surrounds projections of reserve enlistments and losses, however, further steps beyond the recommended pay increase may be necessary. Any further steps should await the results of experience with higher pay during the next few years.

In that transition period, recruiting potential for the reserves will be substantially enhanced by the large flow of servicemen being separated now. Prior service enlistments, as we saw in table 9-X, are expected to be significantly higher in the 1971-73 period than they will later be for the stabilized force. As a result, the require-

TABLE 9–XV.—Projections of non-prior service reserve enlistments, FY 1970–80

[thousands]

Fiscal Year	Manpower pool, age 17–21	Number of enlistments		
		A[1]	B[2]	C[3]
1970	9,253	86.1	92.5	101.8
1971	9,451	87.9	94.5	104.0
1972	9,715	90.3	97.2	106.9
1973	9,941	92.5	99.4	109.4
1974	10,171	94.6	101.7	111.9
1975	10,343	96.2	103.4	113.8
1976	10,485	97.5	104.9	115.3
1977	10,673	99.3	106.7	117.4
1978	10,726	99.8	107.3	118.0
1979	10,781	100.3	107.8	118.6
1980	10,791	100.4	107.9	118.7

[1] Manpower pool multiplied by (.00696) x $(1.436)^{0.8}$. The increase in drill pay is 43.6 percent in the first 4 years.
[2] Manpower pool multiplied by (.00696) x $(1.436)^{1}$.
[3] Manpower pool multiplied by (.00696) x $(1.436)^{1.25}$.

TABLE 9–XVI.—Reserve strengths and required and projected civilian enlistments,* FY 1977
[thousands]

Active force	Volunteer reserve	Required enlistments	Modified reserve	Required enlistments
2,250	712	97	632	82
2,500	786	106	696	89

Projected enlistments	
A[1]	99
B[2]	107
C[3]	117

* Reserve strength scaled to active strength; "modified" strength is after possible reductions discussed in requirements section. Strengths and enlistments omit the "2x6" program.

[1] If enlistment rate is $(0.00696) \times (1.436)^{0.8} = 0.0093$.

[2] If enlistment rate is $(0.00696) \times (1.436)^1 = 0.0100$.

[3] If enlistment rate is $(0.00696) \times (1.436)^{1.25} = 0.0110$.

ment for civilian enlistments will be well within recruiting capabilities in the early years.

This can be seen in FY 1972, for example, when extremely high losses are expected. The currently planned reserve enlisted strength for FY 1971 is 865,000 in the paid-drill category. That strength is higher than the largest force level considered in our analysis, but our study indicates that even that level could be maintained in FY 1972 with volunteers. The re-enlistment rate is expected to reach 9.2 percent by that year, so that an estimated 79,600 men would re-enlist. Prior-service gains would number 81,800. Losses are estimated at 243,000. To maintain level strength would therefore require 81,600 civilian enlistments (losses less re-enlistments and prior service gains). Using the most conservative evaluation of the effects of the proposed pay increase, we have estimated that 99,000 civilians can be persuaded to enlist.

CHAPTER 10

The Standby Draft

Heeding its directive, the Commission has considered "what standby machinery for the draft will be required in the event of a national emergency." The Commission recommends that legislation be enacted to provide, once an all-volunteer force is in effect:

1. A register of all males who might be conscripted when essential for national security.
2. A system for selection of inductees.
3. Specific procedures for the notification, examination, and induction of those to be conscripted.
4. An organization to maintain the register and administer the procedures for induction.
5. That a standby draft system can be invoked only by resolution of Congress at the request of the President.

Because there have been several recent studies of the operation of the Selective Service System, we have not undertaken a re-examination of that subject. Instead, we have formulated our recommendations for standby draft machinery in fairly general terms, which would be consistent with a wide range of specific systems.

Clearly the task of creating and maintaining a state of military preparedness capable of dealing with threats to the nation's security is a vital one. The nation's military readiness is both actual and potential: active-duty personnel are prepared to act instantaneously; able-bodied but untrained and unorganized civilian males are potential servicemen. This spectrum of manpower can be divided into three groups in descending order of their state of readiness: (1) active-duty personnel, (2) reserves, and (3) civilians. In planning standby draft machinery, it is important to recognize that conscription is relevant only to the civilian population.

The rationale for providing a standby draft is the possible urgent need for the nation to act quickly. It is clear, however, that a standby draft will not supply effective military forces in being. All it can provide is a basis for acquiring eligible manpower who must be trained, organized, and equipped. Effective forces can be available only to the extent that men are organized, trained, and equipped prior to an emergency. Under current military policy, should a crisis arise, it is the function of the Reserves to provide the first stage in the expansion of effective forces. They are organized and at least partly trained and equipped; hence they can be operationally ready in a shorter time than new forces. The function of a standby draft is to provide manpower resources for the second stage of expansion in effective forces.

Much thought lies behind the recommendation that Congressional approval be required to invoke conscription. An important issue of national policy is obviously involved. The alternative is to endow the Office of the President with the independent power to call for activation of the standby machinery. This has been rejected for several reasons.

Conscription should be used only when the size of forces required for the security of the nation cannot be supplied by the existing system. If Congressional approval is made a prerequisite to the use of conscription, the necessity for legislative action will guarantee public discussion of the propriety of whatever action is under consideration. If discussion yields a reasonable consensus, the nation's resolve will be clearly demonstrated and made less vulnerable to subsequent erosion. If a consensus sufficient to induce Congress to activate the draft cannot be mustered, the President would see the depth of national division *before,* rather than after, committing U.S. military power.

A standby system which authorizes the President to invoke the draft at his discretion would capture the worst of two worlds. On the one hand, it would make it possible for the President to become involved in military actions with a minimum of public debate and popular support. On the other hand, once the nation was involved, especially in a prolonged limited conflict, the inequities of the draft would provide a convenient rallying point for opposition to the policy being pursued.

It is important to emphasize that Congress has not been reluctant to enact a draft when the President has requested it. In the first World War, the United States declared war on April 1, 1917, the draft law was requested by President Wilson on April 7, and it was signed into law on May 18. Prior to World War II a draft bill was introduced into Congress on June 20, 1940, endorsed by the President on August 2, passed on September 14, and signed into law September 16. When the Korean War broke out on June 24, 1950, debate on extension of the selective service law had been underway for some months. Congress promptly discontinued debate and extended the law for one year on July 9.

Because of the loss of personal freedom and the inequities inherent in conscription, the draft should be resorted to only in extreme situations. If the Office of the President has the power to use the draft, there will be pressures to do so when circumstances do not warrant it. The viability of an all-volunteer force ultimately depends upon the willingness of Congress, the President, the Department of Defense, and the military services to maintain (1) competitive levels of military compensation, (2) reasonable qualification standards, and (3) attractive conditions of military service. Under foreseeable circumstances, such as serious budget constraints, there is a danger that inaction by one or another of these parties might force the President to resort to conscription when it is not really necessary. If Congressional approval is made a prerequisite to use of the draft, the danger of using it unnecessarily or by default will be much reduced.

One of the fundamental principles embodied in the Constitution is that taxes are to be levied only by Congress. Since conscription is a form of taxation, the power to conscript is the power to tax. Therefore, it is in keeping with the intent of the Constitution to require Congressional approval for the activation of the standby draft.

Finally, requiring Congressional approval for activation of a standby draft will have little or no effect on the time required for the nation to bring effective military power to bear when needed. To repeat: conscription does not provide the nation with military forces in being. Effective flexibility in response to crisis can be achieved only to the extent that forces are already partly or wholly organized, trained, and equipped. The draft is a vehicle for supplying men for gradual expansion, not for meeting sudden challenges. This has been true, for example, in Vietnam. Under our standby proposal, the delay introduced in expanding the forces with conscripts cannot exceed the time it takes for Congress to act. In practice the time lost will be even less: preparations for organizing, training, and equipping recruits can proceed simultaneously with Congressional action.

Maximum Size of an All-Volunteer Force

No estimate has been attempted of the maximum size of a force that could be provided on a voluntary basis. When it is posed in this general form, the question of maximum size is not a meaningful one. The number of individuals who will serve voluntarily depends on a variety of factors, more or less subject to control, which change over time. One factor is the specific set of circumstances which dictate the expansion of forces. When the threat to national security is clearly serious, as it was after Pearl Harbor, volunteers will be plentiful. For a limited conflict in a distant and alien land, there will be less enthusiasm. Willingness to volunteer also depends on the character and terms of military service, on casualty rates, and on the public esteem such service enjoys. Most importantly, the flow of volunteers depends upon the level of military compensation.

Pay is important because it leads to more relevant questions regarding the size of the voluntary force which can be sustained. Other things being equal, if it is indeed true that higher military compensation will result in more enlistments, the question of the maximum size of a volunteer force becomes one of how high the level of military compensation should be. Ultimately, each of us faces the question: how heavily are we willing to tax ourselves to pay for a volunteer force? The question of the maximum size of a volunteer military force is at bottom political and not economic. Conscription cannot produce more manpower than already exists. The constraint is political, and it is imposed by the reluctance of voters generally to incur higher taxes even though they want forces large enough to guarantee their security.

Whatever the ultimate limitations on the size of a voluntary force, some relatively large forces have been assembled on such a basis—for example, the Union forces in the Civil War. By the middle of 1862, the North, without conscription, had raised a force of approximately 670,000 men, the vast majority of whom had made three-year commitments. This was 15 percent of the estimated male population, age 18 to 39, of the Union states. During World War I, Great Britain relied on volunteers until 1916. By that time, England had raised an active duty force of nearly 2.7 million men, or 35 percent of her age 18 to 40 male population cohort.

Such examples are by no means conclusive, but they do suggest that conscription is not necessarily required for conflicts comparable in scale to those the United States has fought since World War II. The maximum active duty force levels reached during the Korean and Vietnamese Wars were 3.7 million and 3.6 million respectively. The Korean War force represented 15 percent of the male population age 18 to 39 in 1952, and the Vietnam War force represented 12.4 percent of the male population age 18 to 39 in 1968. In prosecuting those wars with conscripts, the nation imposed a heavy tax on a small segment of the population. In all, 5.8 million men saw service during the Korean War and 6.0 million during the Vietnam War. In neither case was a serious attempt made to expand the forces with volunteers, and in the Vietnam War little use was made of the Reserves.

Historically, whenever conscription has been used, military pay has fallen further behind comparable civilian earnings and, as a result, enlistments have inevitably been discouraged. The more conscription is used, the less incentive there is to maintain military pay (especially for those in the lower ranks) at levels sufficient to attract volunteers. This inverse correlation between conscription and military pay (and therefore volunteerism) is illustrated by the data in table 10-I which compares military pay and allowances to manufacturing earnings at different dates in our history.

In the future, serious consideration should be given to steps which would facilitate the expansion of forces through voluntary means before invoking conscription. In particular, whenever expansion of forces is required to meet a limited emergency, Congress and the President should give serious consideration to enacting significant permanent or temporary increases in military compensation.

TABLE 10–I.—Comparison of annual military enlisted earnings with average annual earnings in manufacturing

Period	Annual military pay and allowances [1]	Manufacturing earnings [2]	Ratio	Percent of forces drafted
Civil War (1865) ...	$ 427 [3]	$ 410	1.041	2
Spanish-American War (1898)	444	394	1.127	0
World War I (1918) .	870	980	.888	59
World War II (1945)	1,587	2,469	.643	61
Korean War (1952) .	2,584	3,721	.694	27
1960	3,034	5,020	.604	15
1965	3,567	6,130	.581	16

[1] Figures include basic pay and value of quarters, food, and clothing but not medical care, insurance benefits, special pays, or income tax exemptions.

[2] Sources:

Civil War—Long estimates average annual earnings in manufacturing in 1860 at $297 (Table 14, p. 42) and a 38 percent increase in average daily wage rates by 1865 (Table 7, p. 25). See Long, *Wages and Earnings in the United States 1860–1890* (New York: National Bureau of Economic Research, 1960).

Spanish-American War—See Table 10 (p. 33) in Rees, *Real Wages in Manufacturing, 1890–1914* (New York: National Bureau of Economic Research, 1968).

World War I—Average Annual Earnings of Manufacturing Wage Earners (Historical Statistics, Series D 605).

1945–65—Average annual earnings per full-time employee in manufacturing, adjusted for unemployment.

[3] This figure does not include the large bounty payments or payments rendered for substitutes.

CHAPTER 11

Budgetary Implications

A major share of our research has been devoted to estimating the budget increases that will be required to sustain an all-volunteer force. The results of that effort are summarized in tables 11-I and 11-II.

Table 11-I presents our estimates of the additional expenditures that will be required to put our recommendations into effect in FY 1971.

Each of these sources of increased budget expenditures is discussed elsewhere in this report.

Table 11-II summarizes the average budget increases required to sustain all-volunteer forces with the same effective strengths as the 2.0, 2.25, 2.5, and 3.0 million man mixed forces for FY 1977 through FY 1979. We have chosen the period 1977 through 1979 as fairly representing the differences in budget requirements for the mixed and all-volunteer forces, because at that time accession requirements will have stabilized, and most of the savings resulting from an all-volunteer force will have taken effect. All of the comparisons are made in constant 1970 dollars; that is, there is no allowance for inflation. The pay profiles used to compute total pay and allowances are those set forth in chapter 5. For all of the mixed forces, we have used the estimated pay for FY 1970, which includes an across-the-board increase of 8 percent. For the 2.0, 2.25, and 2.5 million man all-volunteer force, we have used the proposed pay profile shown in table 5-III. The 3.0 million man volunteer force requires a further pay increase both for first term personnel and for those serving beyond the first term. A more detailed discussion of the method used to derive these estimates is set forth in appendix A.

TABLE 11–I.—Additional budget expenditures for all-volunteer force, FY 1971
[billions]

	Expenditure
Basic pay increase	$2.68
Proficiency pay	.21
Reserve pay increase	.15
Additional Medical Corps expense	.12
Recruiting, ROTC, and misc.	.08
Total	3.24
Less added Federal income tax	.54
Net addition to budget	2.70

TABLE 11–II.—Additional budget expenditures for all-volunteer force, FY 1977–79 average
[billions]

	2.0 Force	2.25 Force	2.5 Force	3.0 Force
Basic pay increase	$1.58	$1.86	$2.24	$5.09
Reserves	.13	.17	.24	.44
Proficiency pay	—	—	.14	.21
Medical	.13	.16	.16	.20
Miscellaneous	.08	.08	.08	.08
Total	1.92	2.27	2.86	6.02
Less turnover related savings [1]	—.16	—.19	—.32	—.50
Total net of turnover related costs	1.76	2.08	2.54	5.52
Less additional Federal income tax [2]	—.29	—.34	—.42	—.97
Net budget increase	1.47	1.74	2.12	4.55

[1] These are savings from reduced turnover over and above the direct pay and allowance savings that accrue as a result of force reductions.

[2] These are the additional Federal income taxes that will be collected as a result of the increased basic pay and other additional compensation paid to members of the active duty and reserve forces. They should properly be deducted in calculating the incremental expense for an all-volunteer force.

CHAPTER 12

Objections
to an All-Volunteer Force

Critics argue that elimination of the draft will adversely affect our society or our armed forces. Their main objections are: (1) an all-volunteer force will become isolated from society and threaten civilian control; (2) isolation and alienation will erode civilian respect for the military and hence dilute its quality; (3) an all-volunteer force will be all-black or dominated by servicemen from low-income backgrounds; (4) an all-volunteer force will lead to a decline in patriotism or in popular concern about foreign policy; (5) an all-volunteer force will encourage military adventurism.

There are several compelling reasons why an all-volunteer force will not have the dire consequences some predict.

First, an all-volunteer armed force will not affect the institutional framework within which the Department of Defense and the military services now operate. The system of manpower recruitment is only a small part of that framework. An all-volunteer force does not impinge on the constitutional roles of the President, who will remain Commander-in-Chief; or the civilian service secretaries, who will remain responsible to him; or Congress, which will continue as an independent legislative and budgetary overseer. The change from a mixed volunteer/conscript force to an all-volunteer force maintains intact the legal structures that define the role and status of the military services.

Second, this structure rests on deeply rooted and widely held values. Americans firmly believe in a clearly defined and limited military role, a belief derived from the Anglo-American heritage of individual freedom and democratic political processes. Defense of personal rights and liberties against all threats, foreign and domestic, has been a constant theme in English and American history. The English established parliamentary control over the military through the Glorious Revolution in 1688. The authors of the United States Constitution recognized that military forces were necessary, but they carefully circumscribed their role. They provided that the President be the Commander-in-Chief of the forces and gave the Congress the power to raise and support armies. Civilian control of the military has concerned every generation of Americans since 1776 and this concern remains high today.

In 1940, when peacetime conscription was first proposed in the United States, Senator Vandenburg reminded the Senate of these long-held attitudes and traditions:

"I am opposed to tearing up one hundred and fifty years of American history and tradition, in which none but volunteers have entered the peacetime Armies and Navies of the United States, unless there is valid reason to believe that this reliance in 1940 has become a broken reed for the first time in a century and a half.

"There must have been sound reasons all down the years why our predecessors in the Congress always consistently and relentlessly shunned this thing which we are now asked to do. These reasons must have been related in some indispensable fashion to the fundamental theory that peacetime military conscription is repugnant to the spirit of democracy and the soul of Republican institutions, and that it leads in dark directions. That certainly is my view."

More recently, President Eisenhower reminded the nation of these considerations in his Farewell Address:

"In the councils of government, we must guard against the acquisition of unwarranted influence, whether sought or unsought, by the military-industrial complex. The potential for the disastrous rise of misplaced power exists and will persist.

"We must never let the weight of this combination endanger our liberties or democratic processes. We should take nothing for granted. Only an alert and knowledgeable citizenry can compel the proper meshing of the huge industrial and military machinery of defense with our peaceful methods and goals, so that security and liberty may prosper together."

In short, however the armed forces are recruited, a watchful population will continue to be the strongest force limiting the influence of the military in American society.

Third, there is much evidence that our society has more to gain than to fear from an all-volunteer force. Throughout its history, the United States has relied on volunteer military forces, resorting to conscription only in time of clear danger. Prior to 1948 conscription was abandoned after each major war and voluntary recruitment reinstated. Only in the past twenty years has the United States used the draft to raise a standing military force. During the long periods of entirely voluntary recruitment the United States never experienced a threat to civilian control from the military. These voluntary military forces were able to accomplish successfully the military tasks required of them. The rush of volunteers at the outbreak of every war demonstrates that a voluntary military did not produce a decline in patriotism. Nor is there evidence in our history that voluntary forces encouraged military adventurism. Our national experience strongly indicates that a volunteer force is likely to promote civilian control of the military, improve the quality of the armed forces, foster continued patriotism and help avoid military adventurism.

Lastly, the manpower policies of an all-volunteer force will largely maintain the existing qualitative composition of the armed forces. This conclusion is based on an analysis of the main alternatives available to us for recruiting military manpower. We have made projections of two future forces—one a mixed volunteer-conscript force, the other an all-volunteer armed force. In comparing the two alternative forces, we use four categories: the career force, true enlistees in their first tour of duty, draft motivated enlistees in their first tour, and draftees.

The career force contains men voluntarily serving beyond any period of obligated service. True enlistees are men who would have joined even if there were no draft. Draft motivated enlistees are men who say they would probably not have joined if there were no draft. Draftees are, of course, men inducted under Selective Service procedures. Table 12-I shows the number of enlisted men in each of the categories for the two alternative 2.5 million man future forces. The table shows that 83 percent of the mixed force will be serving voluntarily.

TABLE 12–I.—Composition of mixed and volunteer enlisted forces, 1980 [millions of men]

	Volunteer force	Mixed force
First-term force		
Draftees	None	.193 (9%)
Draft induced volunteers ...	None	.182 (8%)
True volunteers	1.079 (52%)	.925 (43%)
Career force—volunteers	1.010 (48%)	.846 (40%)
Total	2.089 (100%)	2.146 (100%)

Since career men and true volunteers in the mixed force will remain in a volunteer force, the potential differences in the two forces are mostly limited to the kind of men who are draft induced volunteers or draftees in the present mixed force.

Draft motivated volunteers are men who object less to military service than the men who are drafted. A potential draftee is presented with a forced choice. He can be drafted into the Army for two years or he can enlist in the service of his choice and get a better chance of serving in the branch and occupation he prefers. Enlistment generally requires additional time in service—one year extra in the Army, two extra years in the Navy and Air Force. Draftees are not willing to serve this extra time. But draft motivated volunteers are willing to trade extra time in uniform for preferred service. These draft motivated volunteers are the type who will find service in an all-volunteer force attractive. Improved compensation and better conditions of service will appeal to the men who would otherwise volunteer to avoid the draft. The major quantitative difference between the projected all-volunteer force and the projected mixed volunteer-conscript force is, therefore, the presence of 193,000 draftees in the latter, nine percent of the enlisted force.

Further, the qualitative standards for entry into the two alternative forces will be the same. Identical mental, physical and moral standards will act to reduce differences in the types of men who man the two forces. Men who will not qualify to enter the mixed force will also not qualify for the all-volunteer force. For example, some 30 percent of America's young men do not presently qualify for military service. A disproportionate share of these men come from a low income environment. These men will continue to be ineligible for military service whether or not they are attracted to military life.

Raising first-term military pay will increase the attractiveness of the military more to young men with higher earnings potential than to young men with lower earnings potential. For those who have very poor civilian alternatives even the present low level of first-term pay is relatively attractive. In either the mixed force or the all-volunteer force, men who have very poor civilian alternatives and who meet the military's standards will be able to enlist and re-enlist. But the low first-term pay of the present mixed force is a real obstacle to recruiting men who have better civilian alternatives. Increasing first-term pay for the all-volunteer force removes this obstacle and should increase the flow of qualified enlistees. In spite of low first-term pay an estimated 140,000 high-school graduates entered the military as true volunteers during 1968. Higher first-term pay certainly would have attracted some of the remaining 1.2-million male high-school graduates who either entered the labor force or continued their education.

The men attracted to an all-volunteer force will not necessarily make military service their career. In fact, about 65 percent of the men who enter the all-volunteer force will leave after a single tour of duty. We estimate that turnover in the all-volunteer force will be three-quarters of the turnover in a comparable mixed force. As table 12-I shows, 52 percent of the men in the projected voluntary force will be first-termers—only slightly less than the estimated 60 percent in the comparable mixed force.

The all-volunteer force will resemble a mixed volunteer and conscript force in other ways. In the important area of officer recruitment, the majority of new officers in the all-volunteer force will come from ROTC, direct appointments and officer candidate school. Each year the military will continue to draw new leaders into the service from the same sources as it does today. Most of these men will enter at the bottom and advance to higher levels just as officer personnel do today.

Because we do not expect major changes in the composition of the armed forces, we do not expect major changes in the relationship between the armed forces and the rest of society.

Beyond these general considerations, we felt obliged to study several specific questions to insure that our conclusions were valid. Assuming the change to an all-volunteer force might affect the relations between the armed forces and society, would it result in undesirable separation? How might the change affect the racial composition of the forces? What might be the consequences of a reduced flow of veterans from the forces into society? How might the end of the draft and reliance on all-volunteer forces affect the foreign policy decision-making process? Much of the opposition to an all-volunteer force arises because such questions have not been carefully explored.

Concerns about the all-volunteer force are often expressed in emotionally charged terms—"mercenaries"—and rely on leaps of the imagination to close the gaps where evidence is lacking. It is easy to conjure up the threat of a more powerful military establishment which would gain unwarranted influence within the government, until one hears other voices claiming the opposite—namely, that isolation of the military will lead to reduced influence and a less effective force. Through these (and other) objections runs the assertion that the military and the rest of society will be "alienated."

Isolation and Civilian Control

The long-established institutional framework, firm public attitudes, and the similarity of the future forces with or without conscription will help prevent separation between the armed forces and society if the United States adopts an all-volunteer force. Still, critics feel that the high turnover of manpower generated by the Selective Service System is a healthy phenomenon. The flow of men into and out of the armed forces is thought to generate a link between the services and civilian society that will be weakened or lost with an all-volunteer force. It is claimed that the constant inflow of civilian draftees with limited commitment to the military guards against the growth of a separate military ethos. It is further claimed that the constant outflow of veterans to society makes society more informed, more patriotic, and more alert to threats to national life.

Concern about isolation of the military is heightened by the knowledge that the men in an all-volunteer force would be self-selected rather than chosen by their draft boards. The change, some say, will result in an Army composed of undesirable psychological types, men inclined to use force and violence to solve problems. A mercenary army might develop. The men in the military might come to serve the military's interests against society, leading eventually to loss of society's control over the armed forces. Isolation and alienation could also operate on civilian society. As the military grew apart from the rest of society, interest in military matters would diminish and anti-military attitudes would develop. This would make it difficult to attract high quality men into the armed forces and the military's stature would fall further. A cycle of anti-militarism and falling prestige would ensue. Both the quality of military leadership and the effectiveness of the military as a fighting force would deteriorate. The experience of other nations is sometimes cited to support fears of such undesirable consequences.

We have examined the issues raised by those who fear potential alienation of the armed forces. Some are mutually contradictory. For example, an all-volunteer force cannot both strengthen and weaken the influence of the armed forces. We do not believe that an all-volunteer force such as we recommend will become isolated or alienated from society.

Those who fear greater alienation from voluntary recruiting exaggerate the difference between volunteer and conscripted forces. We have already pointed out that the men in both forces will be largely the same types. Moreover, the turnover of the volunteer force will be three-fourths as large as if conscription is retained. At a force level of 2.5 million men the volunteer force must attract 325,000 men, the conscripted force 440,000 men. Further, the men who join the volunteer force will not all become long service professionals. An estimated 215,000 men will leave after serving a single tour. As a result, about half the men in the volunteer force will be in their first tour of duty. The large infusion of new men will help insure that neither force becomes isolated from society.

The charge that the United States' armed forces will become "mercenaries" is easiest to answer. The term implies a single motive—monetary reward—which precludes patriotism and all other motives for service. It is usually applied to those who serve a foreign power. We simply cannot take the charge seriously. Why should an all-volunteer force be a mercenary force when our local police, F.B.I. agents, and federal marshals, all entirely voluntary, are not? Changes in compensation and conditions of service for the all-volunteer force will enhance the attractiveness of the armed forces for citizens who will serve for a variety of reasons. Many factors affect the choice between military and civilian opportunities, and pay is weighed along with the chance for interesting work, living conditions, travel, opportunities for promotion and others.

To suggest that men who enlist to serve their country do so only for pay is to demean the hundreds of thousands who voluntarily serve today. More than half of all the men in today's forces are true volunteers. This includes one-third of the men with less than four years service. Given today's first-term pay levels, these men must be motivated by other considerations, including a high sense of dedication to their country. Whatever motivates these first-term men will not disappear simply because the draft is no longer used to compel other men to serve and because conditions of service improve. Nor should we expect that the recommended pay increases will diminish the demonstrated dedication of the career force. On the contrary, patriotism is now weakened by the fact that society initially underpays men who volunteer and generally treats military service as an activity which men will undertake only if compelled to do so.

The charge that the all-volunteer force will be manned by "hired killers" obsessed with violence is as empty as the talk of "mercenaries." Such men—assuming they exist in significant numbers—are free to join the present mixed force. If anything, discipline of the violence-prone would be enhanced in a fully professional volunteer force.

As for the feared possibility of military intervention in political matters, this occurs when civilian political leadership is weak and indecisive or when its legitimacy is called into question. Those nations which have experienced military interference in political affairs suffer ills entirely unrelated to the presence or absence of conscripts in the ranks. Furthermore, such interventions usually arise from the officer corps. In the two major nations which have relied on volunteer forces throughout most of their modern history—the United States and the United Kingdom—it is difficult to find anything remotely resembling military intervention.

The modern history of Europe and Latin America reveals no evidence that all-volunteer forces are more likely to overthrow civilian leadership. But, major direct military interventions in political affairs are not the only concern of those who oppose an all-volunteer force as a threat to civilian control of the military. They also fear that the military will acquire excessive political and social influence. These fears appear groundless. An all-volunteer force will not have any more influence on the President, Congress or the rest of society than the military now possesses. In fact, to the extent size alone matters, the impact of an all-volunteer force will be less since it will be somewhat smaller than a mixed force of equal effectiveness. An all-volunteer force will have a larger budget, but the additional funds will be used for compensation and will not provide more control over real resources.

Elimination of the draft will also reduce somewhat the military's influence over the use of manpower resources in the civilian sector. The Selective Service System frankly acknowledges that it uses the draft to direct potential draftees into activities it regards as vital to the nation:

> The deferment of men from military service to pursue civilian activities in the national interest has always been a function of Selective Service. The prospect of deferment has had the effect of influencing men to pursue such activities.
>
> The spectrum of skills vital to the nation's capacity to survive has steadily broadened. Its limits cannot be foreseen. It embraces many civilian activities as well as service in uniform. Particularly since the beginning of the "space age" the breadth of the concept of what constitutes "service" in defense has been difficult to fix. But it has been equally apparent that the fullest development and wisest utilization by citizens of their capabilities is vital to the nation.

In making decisions about manpower allocation, the Selective Service System operates independent of any direct Congressional review. This "channeling" process gives deferments for defense related work and not for otherwise similar non-defense work. The return to an all-volunteer force would end this practice, and to that extent limit the military's influence on the setting of social priorities in America.

On balance the elimination of conscription may slightly reduce the influence of the military, but the effect is so small as to be negligible.

Behind fears that the military's political power would be enlarged lies a basic concern that an all-volunteer force would develop its own rigid ethos. Even if the military did not have increased political power, some fear it would use the power it possessed in undesirable ways. Again, this fear assumes a greatly exaggerated difference between an all-volunteer and a mixed force.

The officer corps exercises the dominant influence on military values. Elimination of the draft will not significantly alter its composition. Officers will continue to be recruited from all over the nation and from a variety of socio-economic backgrounds. Further, the change to an all-volunteer force will have no effect on top leadership, since these men have always been professionals. There is little evidence that the views of enlisted men have a significant impact on their thinking and even less evidence that this impact depends upon how enlisted men are recruited. If there is a separate military ethos, it will persist in a mixed as well as an all-volunteer force.

Moreover, it is by no means clear that a problem exists at all. There is now significant interaction between the military and the rest of society. The military is not isolated from the mass media which permeate all walks of life. Also, the forces contain a wide variety of specialists, not only in air, sea and ground combat, but also in all branches of engineering and science, in computer applications, medicine and dentistry, law, aviation, personnel management, ship building, and others. These men are often in daily contact with their fellow professionals in the civilian sector. Much specialist and officer training takes place in the civilian sector. The Defense Department employs more than one million civilians, and many officers serve tours of duty which require daily contact with the business community, academic institutions, and other civilian organizations.

If the present degree of military and civilian interaction is inadequate, conscription does not solve the problem. The solution lies in taking further steps to reduce the separation between the military and the rest of society. Many of the benefits provided in-kind to military personnel increase that separation. A serviceman can live on a base, shop in the commissary and post exchange, send his children to a school filled with children whose parents are also in the military, and have his family's medical needs attended to in a military hospital. If more military compensation were paid in cash and less of it in-kind, the military might be less isolated from the rest of society. Also, more of the training and education of military personnel could be civilianized; and, as suggested elsewhere in this report, medical services could be civilianized. An aggressive expansion in the use of lateral entry, especially in the officer corps, would provide leaders less identified with any prevailing military ethos. These are some steps which might be taken if the nation desires a closer identification between military and civilian values. However, they may have an adverse effect on morale in the military. By working and living together, servicemen develop a rapport which is very important in combat. One cost of having more civil-military integration may be a less effective defense establishment.

Isolation and Military Quality

While some worry that an all-volunteer force will increase the power of the military, others believe it will lead to the deterioration of the military. They see the end of conscription as causing public neglect, significant reductions in the defense budget, a general decline in the prestige of military service, and a reduced quality of military personnel. In fact, the effect of the all-volunteer force should be the reverse of this gloomy picture. As it stands today the draft is a major source of antagonism toward the military, which erodes public support of the armed services. Because the draft is unnecessary, an all-volunteer force offers an obvious opportunity to curb the growth of anti-militaristic sentiment.

Of course, civil-military relations will never be uncontroversial. They have not been so in the past, whether manpower has been raised by conscription or voluntarism. The military have a distinct and separate set of responsibilities of fundamental importance to the survival of American society. Military leaders seek assurance that they will be able to accomplish successfully the tasks they may be called upon to do. Uncertainty about potential threats and our ability to cope with them leads to differing judgments about the size of forces required. These differences bring about conflict between the demands of the military and the demands of other groups in our society and will do so regardless of whether there is a draft.

The resolution of this conflict will vary depending on the public's evaluation of national priorities. During the 1930's defense expenditures averaged one percent of Gross National Product, but from 1955 to 1964 they averaged nine percent of Gross National Product. The strength of our armed forces is based on fundamental public attitudes toward national defense. No doubt the shift to an all-volunteer force will have some effect on those attitudes. Those who no longer face the threat of conscription and those who oppose the draft on moral grounds are likely to feel less hostile toward the military, while those whose taxes are increased may be displeased. On balance, it is difficult to see which of these factors will predominate.

More importantly, it seems clear that neither factor is likely to have very much effect. Since World War II our peacetime armed forces have been consistently supported at levels unparalleled in our history. This can hardly be explained by the fact that we have also had conscription during these years. The public has supported the maintenance of large forces because it has felt that they were essential to national security. The change from a mixed force of volunteers and conscripts to an all-volunteer force will not dramatically change that feeling.

In recent years military service has been scorned and condemned by some Americans. No doubt, the Vietnam War is partly responsible, but the draft has also contributed to the military's unpopularity. Young men are inevitably skeptical about a career in an organization which has to use compulsion to obtain recruits. Moreover, the low pay implies that society places little value on a soldier. The termination of the draft should immediately enhance the prestige of enlisted service. The knowledge that those in the armed forces have freely chosen to serve their country cannot but improve their image—in their own eyes as well as in the eyes of society. Our recommendations regarding military compensation have been discussed earlier. They should also go a long way toward improving the image of a military career and they are aimed at maintaining the quality of military personnel. Many of our recommendations for increasing the efficiency of military personnel management will also enhance the image of military life. Making the terms of obligated service for enlisted men the same as those for officers, vesting retirement benefits, encouraging lateral entry and similar changes will operate to reduce the differences between military and civilian careers. Military careers will become more professional and avoid the stigma of being an unpleasant task that some men must be forced to do temporarily.

The return to an all-volunteer armed force should improve the "quality" of military life. Conscription enables the military to ignore individual dignity and desire, secure in the knowledge that the draft will replace those who do not like the military system. The entire military "atmosphere"—the approach to training, discipline, and treatment of individuals—must be re-examined. In the modern army at most one-third of the men serve in infantry or ground combat units, and the others serve in technical, administrative and logistical billets. The appeal and utility of military occupational training can be improved by greater recognition that some individuals do not need the kind of training traditionally given all recruits as potential infantrymen. Assignment policies which minimize family separation and which reduce the frequency of duty changes and moves will also make military life more attractive.

Elimination of conscription will also affect the American officer corps even though its recruits have always been volunteers. The draft induces many men to volunteer for service as officers to avoid being inducted as enlisted men. Thus the prestige of military service has been hurt by the draft even in the officer corps. Officers as well as enlisted men will benefit from the changes the Commission is recommending. Pay will be increased, particularly for junior officers. Change in conditions of service and in the quality of military life will make military careers more attractive to potential officers.

An Army of the Black?

Members of both the white and Negro communities have expressed concern that the all-volunteer force might fill its enlisted ranks with the poor and the black. This concern is linked to the recognition that to move to a voluntary force requires a substantial increase in first-term military pay. Higher pay, it is said, will increase the attractiveness of military service primarily among lower income groups, where the proportion of Negroes is high. A predominantly black enlisted force might develop. This will result, according to some, in the black and the poor bearing a disproportionate share of the burden of defense. Some whites are concerned with the dangers of having in the community a large number of blacks who have had military training. They fear that these men will participate in domestic disorders and riots.

There is no evidence that the black community would be happy with an increase in the number of blacks in the military. Increasing the attractiveness of the military will draw able young males into the services because other job opportunities are denied them. In most black communities there is a need for able young black males to enter civilian careers, work on community projects, and inspire the young. There is strong evidence to suggest that the black community, more than the white, looks at the "male drain" as extremely costly.

Many of these questions and concerns cannot be answered rationally. Racial attitudes and fears are emotionally based. Solid facts and sound judgments are seldom cures for prejudice. For example, those who fear "domestic disorders" as a result of blacks serving in the military raise such unanswerable questions. To bar blacks from the military because of these fears will not solve the root causes behind domestic disorders. Black participation in the military will neither quiet nor aggravate domestic disorders.

The racial aspects of the relationship between the armed forces and society have been given special consideration by the Commission. We have concluded that the racial composition of the armed forces cannot be fundamentally changed by ending the draft. Even if higher pay appealed only to the "poor," twice as many whites as blacks would be attracted. The proportion of blacks below the poverty line in 1967 was 38 percent while only 11 percent of whites were in the same category. But, in absolute numbers, more than twice as many whites (17.6 million) as blacks (8.3 million) were below the poverty line.

The relevant comparison is between the racial mix of the all-volunteer force and the racial mix of an alternative force of conscripts and volunteers. We conclude that the similar manpower policies of the two forces will result in similar racial composition in the two forces. The mental, physical, and moral standards for enlistment will ensure that neither force recruits an undue proportion from minority groups or the poor. The best estimate of the proportion of blacks in the all-volunteer force is 14.9 percent, compared with 14.1 percent in a mixed force of conscripts and volunteers. In the Army, the proportion of blacks in the volunteer force is 18.8 percent; in the mixed force it is 16.6 percent. At a 2.5 million man force level, only five to ten thousand more blacks will serve in the enlisted component of a volunteer force than in a mixed force.

Our estimates are based on a careful review of all aspects of the racial composition of the armed forces. As a first step, participation by whites and blacks in the military during the 1960's was examined. Second, the detailed projections of the alternative future forces were analyzed to determine the racial mix of the 2.5 million man force in 1980. The number of blacks in either force depends on the number of young black males in the population, their qualifications for military service, the rate at which the qualified enter the military, and the rate at which they re-enlist. Our analysis of these factors is based on data provided by the Department of Defense and the Census Bureau.

Participation of Blacks in Present Forces

Because of racial differences in civilian earnings, even the current levels of military pay are more attractive to blacks than to whites. In 1966, the average annual income of a 24-year-old white high school graduate was $6013, for a black high school graduate the same age average annual income was $4344. In the military, the earnings of the two men would be nearly the same. In spite of this relative attractiveness, the proportion of blacks in the armed forces has been slightly less than the proportion in the U.S. male population.

During the late 1960's, Negroes constituted from 9.0 to 9.5 percent of the total armed force. In June 1969, two percent of the officers were Negro as were 10.5 percent of the total enlisted force as shown in table 12-II. Both in total and in the enlisted component alone, the proportion of Negroes was somewhat less than their proportion (12 percent) in the young male population. Negro participation in the Army in Southeast Asia (11.4

percent) is slightly less than their percentage in the total Army (11.7 percent).

The forces of the 1960's were, of course, mixed forces of volunteers and conscripts. However, the racial composition of these forces is only partially the result of

TABLE 12–II.—Negro participation in the Armed Forces, June 30, 1969 [percent]

	Officer	Enlisted	Total	In SE Asia
Army	3.2	12.8	11.7	11.4
Navy	0.4	5.3	4.8	4.5
Marine Corps .	1.0	11.9	11.0	10.3
Air Force	1.8	10.6	9.2	10.5
DOD total ..	2.0	10.5	9.5	10.4

conscription, since even under the draft a majority of the military are there on a fully voluntary basis. The distinction between the first term force and the career force is helpful in understanding the racial composition of the armed forces. The first term force includes draftees, draft motivated volunteers and true volunteers, men who say they would have volunteered at current pay levels even if there were no draft. The career force includes all men who have voluntarily re-enlisted.

The racial mix among true volunteers in the first term of service and in the career force gives some insight into the racial composition of the all-volunteer force. Table 12-III shows that blacks constituted only 12.7 percent of nearly 1.7 million enlisted men serving voluntarily in 1969. Among true volunteers, blacks are now serving in the armed forces almost exactly in proportion to their numbers in the U.S. population. About one-third of the men in the first term of service are true volunteers. Of these men, 11.6 percent are black. The proportion of blacks in the career force is 13.1 percent—only slightly higher than the percent in the U.S. population. The same holds for women in the military who, of course, serve free of the compulsion of the draft. In all cases, the proportion of blacks is highest in the Army and lowest in the Navy. At present, blacks constitute nearly 20 percent of the Army career enlisted force.

TABLE 12–III.—Blacks, as a percent of enlisted true volunteers in the 1969 Armed Forces

	Male			Female
	First term	Career	Total	Total
Army	16.4	19.2	17.7	15.4
Navy	6.0	7.0	6.5	6.2
Marine Corps ..	11.8	11.9	11.8	15.1
Air Force	11.4	12.0	11.8	11.1
DOD total ...	11.6	13.1	12.7	11.0

These proportions depend on the racial mix among men entering the two force components. The proportion of blacks in the first term true volunteer force depends on the proportion of blacks among true volunteers entering the military. The proportion of blacks in the career force depends on the proportion of re-enlistees who are black. The data in table 12-IV show blacks as a percent of the men flowing into the career force. (The percentage given in the table should not be confused with re-enlistment rates. Re-enlistment rates are higher for Negroes than for whites, but these depend on the definition of eligibility for re-enlistment. Since eligibility rates are lower for Negroes than for whites, a comparison using re-enlistment rates overstates the proportion of Negroes entering the career force.) The percentage of blacks among those re-enlisting at the end of their first term of service has fallen sharply in recent years. This is largely the result of a sharp decline in the percentage of blacks among first

TABLE 12–IV.—Blacks as a percent of first-term re-enlistments [1]

	1965	1966	1967	1968	1969
Army	22.3	20.7	19.2	14.3	11.8
Navy	6.8	6.4	7.1	6.5	6.8
Marine Corps ...	12.5	11.8	13.4	12.0	12.8
Air Force	15.1	10.9	15.1	13.0	14.0
DOD total	16.3	14.7	14.6	11.9	11.4

[1] Data for 1965 to 1968 are calendar year. Data for 1969 are fiscal year.

term re-enlistees in the Army. The decline in the percentage of blacks re-enlisting will eventually lead to a decline
in the percent of blacks in the Army career force.

In summary, in today's force blacks do not serve disproportionately to their numbers in the population. This
is true for the total force and for the true volunteer component alone. Black participation is highest in the Army,
where about one man in five in the career force is Negro.

Participation of Blacks in Future Forces

Estimating the participation of blacks in the all-volunteer force or the future mixed volunteer and conscript
force requires examination of (1) the projected pool of
young white and black men available for military service,
(2) the ability of these men to meet the mental and
physical standards of the military service, (3) the first
term military participation rates among qualified men of
both races and (4) the re-enlistment behavior of men
in the military. A range of estimates of the proportion of
blacks in the armed forces has been developed by varying
assumptions about qualifications rates, enlistment rates
and re-enlistment rates.

Young men in the 17 to 20 age group are the primary
source of initial enlistments. During the 1970's this pool
will grow by more than a million men. But, since the
white pool will grow at a slower rate than the black pool,
the proportion of blacks available for military service
will increase, as shown in table 12-V. This trend makes it
likely that the proportion of enlisted blacks in either the
all-volunteer force or the mixed force will increase during

**TABLE 12–V.—Trends in the 17–20 male population
[in thousands]**

Year	Black	White	Total	Percent nonwhite
1965	782	5,726	6,508	12.0
1970	998	6,456	7,454	13.4
1975	1,159	7,188	8,347	13.9
1980	1,297	7,358	8,655	15.0
1985	1,195	6,388	7,583	15.8

the 1970's from today's 10.5 percent. These proportions of blacks in the military age population provide a standard for evaluating minority group participation in the alternative future forces.

It is an unfortunate fact that not all these young men will be qualified for military service. The qualifications for service will be retained at today's level in both the all-volunteer force and the alternative mixed force. To be acceptable for military service, young men must meet certain minimum physical, moral, and mental standards. For example, men who score in the lowest 10 percent on the Armed Forces Qualification Test are exempted from military service. The results of examinations of draftees provide an estimate of the overall qualifications of young men for military service. (See table 12-VI.) Clearly, the

TABLE 12–VI.—Preinduction examination acceptance rates [percent]

	1964	1965	1966	1967	1968
White	52.8	60.3	64.8	60.8	59.7
Black	21.7	29.2	42.5	49.9	45.8

proportion of young black men found acceptable for military service in preinduction examinations is lower than the proportion of young whites found acceptable. But just as clearly, the acceptance rate for young blacks is rising rapidly. Acceptance rates for enlistees are higher than for draftees, running better than 90 percent overall. Combining the results for draftees with the higher acceptance rates for similar examinations for enlistees in all services gives an overall acceptability rate of about 73 percent for whites and 53 percent for blacks based on the recent past. Estimates of the qualified black population have been made based on recent experience (53 percent acceptability), and for improved black acceptance rates (63 percent acceptability) and are shown in table 12-VII. The acceptability of young whites has been held constant at 73 percent. Though the proportion of young blacks in the population is growing, their numbers remain relatively small. This limits the number of blacks who will serve in the armed forces.

TABLE 12–VII.—Male population 17–20 qualified for military service

	Qualified black population based on		Qualified white population
	53-percent acceptability	63-percent acceptability	73-percent acceptability
1970	528,490	628,740	4,712,880
1975	614,270	770,170	5,247,240
1980	684,410	817,110	5,371,340
1985	633,350	752,850	4,663,240

The next step in estimating the racial composition of future forces is to determine the numbers of men of both races who can be expected to participate in the first-term force. The all-volunteer force will attract men through higher pay and improved conditions of service. The mixed force would include draftees, draft induced volunteers and true volunteers. Recent experience has been used to estimate the participation of true volunteers in the armed forces and to show how the participation rate is affected by military pay increases. Table 12-VIII gives true volunteers in the first term of service during 1969 as a percent of the qualified male population, 17 to 20. For example, some 51,200 blacks in the Army in their first term of duty would have enlisted even if there had been no draft. In 1969 the qualified black population was about 512,000, so 10 percent of the qualified men were serving as true volunteers.

The rates in table 12-VIII, and similar participation

TABLE 12–VIII.—True volunteer participation rates at current levels of pay

	White (percent)	Black (percent)
Army	5.65	10.00
Navy	3.80	2.18
Marine Corps	2.47	2.96
Air Force	3.46	4.01
DOD total	15.38	19.15

rates for draft induced volunteers have been used to esti-mate volunteer participation in the mixed volunteer and conscript forces. The proportion of blacks among draftees in recent years has been higher than their proportions in the qualified population. During the last five years, Ne-groes constituted only 9.2 percent of the qualified popula-tion but were 14.3 percent of the men actually inducted. Estimates of the proportion of blacks among draftees are based on recent experience and, alternatively, on the as-sumption that blacks are drafted exactly in proportion to their numbers in the qualified population.

Voluntary participation rates depend on the relation-ship between the military compensation and civilian earnings. If military pay is increased relative to civilian earnings, participation rates should increase. The pay in-creases recommended in chapter 5 will result in about a 40 percent increase in first term military pay. But the effect of the increase on black participation rates will be smaller than on white participation rates. Because a larger proportion of the qualified black population is willing to serve at today's relative pay level, the 40 percent increase will attract a smaller percentage of additional black en-trants. For example, studies of Air Force re-enlistments in-dicate that a 10 percent increase in relative pay will increase white re-enlistments by 24 percent but black re-enlistments by only 18 percent. Two assumptions were used in esti-mating the effect of the recommended first term pay in-crease on participation rates. In one case, the percentage increase in the black participation rate was assumed to be three-quarters of the percentage increase in the white participation rate. In the other case, equal percentage in-creases were assumed.

Experience during the 1960's has also been used to estimate the racial composition of the career force. For example, blacks constituted 12.7 percent of the true volun-teers entering the Air Force between 1963 and 1966. When men who entered the Air Force in this cohort made first term re-enlistment decisions, 14.4 percent of the re-enlistees were black. The ratio of these percentages, 1.134, is applied to the estimated first term black proportion to estimate the proportion of blacks in the career force. Thus, if 11.1 percent of the men in the first term service in the

Air Force were black, the percent of blacks in the career force is estimated to be 12.6. The same procedure was used for all services.

These assumptions and estimates yield a variety of estimates of the proportion of blacks in the two alternative 2.5 million man future forces. For the voluntary force, these estimates range from 12.8 percent to 16.0 percent. For the mixed force of conscripts and volunteers the lowest estimate is 12.1 percent and the highest is 15.1 percent. Tables 12-IX and 12-X give the best estimate of the proportion of blacks in the two forces. For both forces, these

TABLE 12–IX.—Estimated racial composition of the enlisted male all-volunteer force in 1980

	White	Black	Total	Percent Negro
Army	671,250	155,850	827,100	18.8
Navy	476,050	42,550	518,600	8.2
Marine Corps	155,150	29,650	184,800	16.0
Air Force	476,200	82,700	558,900	14.8
DOD total	1,778,650	310,750	2,089,400	14.9

TABLE 12–X.—Estimated racial composition of the enlisted male mixed force in 1980

	White	Black	Total	Percent Negro
Army	723,400	144,300	867,700	16.6
Navy	483,750	42,850	526,600	8.1
Marine Corps	154,250	31,950	186,200	17.1
Air Force	481,200	84,200	565,400	14.9
DOD total	1,842,600	303,300	2,145,900	14.1

estimates assume that the proportion of black males qualified for military service rises to 63 percent. For the mixed force, blacks are assumed to be drafted in proportion to their presence in the qualified population. For the all-volunteer force, the effect of the first term military pay increase is assumed to be smaller for blacks than for whites. Given these assumptions, the proportion of blacks in the two forces is nearly equal. The highest estimate for the proportion of blacks in the all-volunteer force, 16.0 percent, occurs when the effect of the pay increase is assumed to be the same for both races. For the mixed force, the highest estimate is 15.1 percent, when blacks are assumed to be drafted in a higher proportion than their numbers in the qualified population, as during the late 1960's.

Even if higher estimates were realized, we would not consider asking the government—including the military—to cut back on hiring blacks, or to set quotas. Government service has traditionally been a major source of employment for blacks. This is as true for blacks with the highest skills and degrees as well as for other levels of training and income. The participation of blacks in municipal, state and national government reflects the confidence blacks have in the government as a "hirer of last resort." Discrimination and segregation in other sectors of society traditionally have persisted long after government policy changed to include blacks. Citizens who are concerned with racial imbalance in this or that sector must work to open opportunities for blacks in all occupations. Then, and only then, will the question of "proportionate representation" be fair.

Veterans in Society

Many Americans are concerned that creation of an all-volunteer force will adversely affect the size and composition of the veteran population. They reason that a system of military recruitment which uses conscription takes many young men from society, exposes them to an important experience, and then rather quickly returns them to civilian life.

Veterans are today a substantial part of American society. In 1968 veterans were 13 percent of the total population, 23 percent of the adult population, and 47 percent of the adult male population. These more than 27 million veterans averaged 44 years in age, and 27 months of active duty. Both their numbers and their ages make the influence of veterans on American life highly significant.

A volunteer system will take fewer recruits, retain them

longer, and return fewer veterans to civilian society. If military experience is beneficial, there would be some loss in the qualities that veterans bring to society—qualities that are attributed to military experience.

Military life is thought to have a discernible and beneficial impact on an individual's capabilities, attitudes, and behavior patterns as they are carried over into the veteran's civilian life. The differences between veterans and non-veterans are described in a variety of ways. Veterans are said to display more patriotism and to be readier to serve our nation. Some argue that veterans are better informed and more concerned about a wide variety of foreign and domestic affairs and, thus, are more alert to threats to the nation. Veterans are alleged to behave differently—to have more self-discipline and to pay greater attention to neatness and hygiene. Veterans are said to do better economically than non-veterans, to participate more in community social and political activities, and, in general, to make better and more productive citizens.

We have studied the effect of an all-volunteer force on the size of the veteran population. In addition, we have examined the effect of military service on men's attitudes toward national security and other contemporary issues to determine whether veterans are different from non-veterans and whether the differences are beneficial.

At any force level, the turnover of military personnel and the consequent annual flow of new veterans will be smaller under an all-volunteer system than under the mixed, conscript-volunteer system. Using an estimate of 15 percent as the enlisted turnover for the volunteer force and 20 percent for the mixed force, about 130,000 fewer veterans would be added annually to the veteran population with the all-volunteer force.

For the next 20 years World War II, Korean War, and Vietnam veterans will dominate the veteran population and therefore the short-run impact of ending the draft will be small. Eventually, lower turnover will mean a smaller veteran population. For example, by adding projected new veteran accessions to the existing veteran population and adjusting for mortality, the present system of conscription will generate a veteran population of 26.3 million by the year 2000. For the same effective force, an all-volunteer force adopted in 1971 would generate 3.2 million fewer veterans over the next 30 years. Veterans as a percentage of the total population would decrease from 13 percent today to about 8 percent in the year 2000 under a mixed conscript-volunteer system and to about 7 percent for an all-volunteer force.

Whatever the exact quantitative effect of a return to an all-volunteer force, if military service instills patriotism and greater awareness of national interests, ending the draft would eventually affect public attitudes about foreign policy and national security matters. Alternatively, if military service does not instill different attitudes then the change in method of recruiting will have no effect. To study the influence of military service on public attitudes we used national opinion surveys on a wide variety of domestic, foreign policy and security issues that also had information on the veteran status of respondents. Military experience proved to be a minor factor in explaining opinion differences. Other characteristics—notably occupation, income, region, education, political party, age, race and other sociological attributes—are far better predictors of attitudes than veteran status. Indeed, there is a significant difference between attitudes of veterans and non-veterans—holding other characteristics constant—on only one matter of contemporary debate—namely, attitudes toward veterans' benefits.

Similarly, the effect of military training on earnings is much more questionable than frequently supposed. Since 1960 over three-quarters of the active military personnel served in jobs that had white-collar or blue-collar civilian counterparts. Yet, only an estimated one-quarter of the men who left the service accepted jobs which they judged to be related to their military service. The figure for the Army, which experiences the highest turnover rate, is 15 percent, the lowest among the services.

As with attitudes, earnings depend on such factors as age, ability, education and race. Gross comparisons of veterans' and non-veterans' incomes are likely to be misleading because men who enter the service are more intelligent, healthier, and have more schooling than those who do not. A meaningful comparison would allow for these factors. Recent studies which have attempted to do this conclude that differences in the earnings between veterans and non-veterans disappear when factors other than military service are considered.

In summary, the belief that two or three years of military service increases earnings or alters opinions is not supported by the evidence. Other experience factors, such as region, education, age, and the more fundamental family and community history, are more significant in shaping a person's earning power and the way he thinks of himself and of his environment. Most of these factors are determined long before military service and are unaffected by it. Whatever qualities veterans bring to their communities —informed judgment or ignorance, patriotism or indifference, self-discipline or personal disarray, community participation or apathy—are qualities that these individuals would probably have displayed without prior military experience.

Effects on Foreign Policy Decision Making

We have heard conflicting concerns about the effect on foreign policy of a return to voluntary recruiting. One view foresees a less militaristic foreign policy as a consequence of the all-volunteer force; the other, more military adventurism.

Those who hold the first opinion believe that an all-volunteer force necessarily will be smaller and less flexible than a force raised by conscription. Therefore the return to voluntary recruiting signals a weakening of the United States' capability to meet its military commitments overseas. The opposing belief is that the greater training and readiness of a volunteer force will offer a tempting military solution to problems which might be better resolved peacefully. Further, those who hold this opinion think that an all-volunteer force would have fewer and weaker links to civilian society, imperiling democratic control of foreign policy decisions. We have considered both of these concerns in the light of our recommendations. Neither provides a valid basis for rejecting the all-volunteer force.

Since World War II, the United States has benefited from an extensive system of defense alliances. Similarly, the security and freedom of our allies depend on United

States' military power. Both the resolve and capability of the United States to continue using its power in the defense of freedom help shape the expectations and actions of friendly governments. Our recommendations are designed to insure that an all-volunteer armed force would be fully consistent with the strategic concepts underlying national security policy.

This Commission has not tried to project the armed forces required to carry out the nation's foreign policy after the transition to an all-volunteer force. The determination of these peacetime force requirements is the responsibility of the Department of Defense and the National Security Council. The Commission has relied on a range of estimates of active duty requirements and developed estimates of the all-volunteer force required to yield the same effective force strength as these equivalent mixed forces of conscripts and volunteers.

In addition to active duty forces, there will be 700,000 to 800,000 trained men in Reserve or National Guard units (assuming a 2.5 million man active duty force). These units furnish a force capable of rapid mobilization, which no draft law can match. Deployment lead times vary from less than a week for some naval units to 6 to 14 weeks for Army units. Under an all-volunteer system, these units will continue to be an important second line of defense. If a crisis situation requires more men than are available in the active and reserve forces, untrained manpower from the civilian pool can be recruited voluntarily or by conscription.

As set forth elsewhere in this report, the Commission recommends that permanent peacetime forces be put on a voluntary basis and that a stand-by draft system be maintained in readiness. We cannot foresee the shape of future threats to the security of the United States, and prudence requires that provision be made for mobilizing civilian manpower by conscription if necessary.

The Commission's recommendations, in summary, provide 1) active duty forces comparable in strength to those currently projected, 2) reserve forces for quick reinforcement of the active forces, and 3) a stand-by draft system as a final measure if large-scale mobilization of untrained men is needed. We believe that these provisions constitute an effective and flexible military manpower policy, and will enhance national security during and after the transition to an all-volunteer force.

We have examined how the return to volunteer forces might affect the decision to use U.S. military power. We conclude that the recommended all-volunteer force will actually increase democratic participation in decisions concerning the use of military force. We reject the fear of increased military aggressiveness or reduced civilian concern following the return to an all-volunteer force.

A decision to use the all-volunteer force will be made according to the same criteria as the decision to use a mixed force of conscripts and volunteers because the size and readiness of the two forces will be quite similar. These military factors are key determinants in any decision to commit forces. Beyond initial commitment, the policy choice between expanding our forces by conscription or by voluntary enlistment is the same for both the all-volunteer force and a mixed force of conscripts and volunteers. The important difference between the two forces lies in the necessity for political debate before returning to conscription. Voluntary enlistments in both alternative forces can be increased by enhancing the attractiveness of military service. If either force is expanded by making military service more attractive, civilian participation obviously will be increased in the process. Increased pay and added fringe benefits will be borne by the general taxpayers, a far more inclusive group than potential draftees and their families. If tax increases are needed or military spending claims priority over other public spending, a broad public debate is likely. Recent history suggests that increased taxes generate far more public discussion than increased draft calls.

With the all-volunteer force, the President can seek authorization to activate the stand-by draft, but Congress must give its consent. With the mixed system, draft calls can be increased by the President. The difference between the two alternatives is crucial. The former will generate public discussion of the use of the draft to fight a war, the latter can be done without such public discussion. If the need for conscription is not clear, such discussion will clarify the issue, and the draft will be used only if public support is widespread.

The claim is made that the ranks of the public attentive

to foreign policy are swelled significantly by those citizens touched by the draft. It is a doubtful notion. The corollary —that public interest in foreign affairs will decrease significantly if voluntarism is adopted—is also doubtful. Volunteers have as many concerned relatives and friends as men who are drafted. Higher educational levels, the diffusion of modern mass communications, and the newsworthiness of compelling national security events assure that foreign affairs will hold the attention of a substantial and growing public, regardless of the method used for procuring military manpower.

When a minority is selected to fight a long and unpopular war, the draft is inevitably a focal point for dissent. Voluntarism would be expected to decrease dissent stemming from the issue of conscription. However, popular dissent usually arises from many issues and reaches the Government along many channels. Ending conscription will close off one of the channels, but it will not end dissent.

Because conscription is a tax in kind, part of the cost of armed forces is hidden when there is a draft. The explicit costs of using military forces are underestimated, with the result that decisions to use the armed forces are made which perhaps would not be made if the true costs were known. The all-volunteer force, by making economic and political costs explicit, should lead to more rational and democratic decisions about the use of military force.

Finally, there is the allegation that political leaders will be more inclined to military adventures if the armed forces are composed entirely of volunteers. This argument is based on three important inferences: (1) an all-volunteer force will be more aggressive than a mixed force; (2) the nation's civilian and military leaders will risk the lives of volunteers with less concern than those of conscripts; and (3) a doubtful foreign commitment could be undertaken and sustained with less popular dissent than if conscripts were used.

Decisions by a government to use force or to threaten the use of force during crises are extremely difficult. Presidents have arrived at such decisions only after consulting a broad range of informed and responsible interests. The high cost of military resources, the moral burden of risking human lives, political costs at home and overseas, and the overshadowing risk of nuclear confrontation—these and other factors enter into such decisions. It is absurd to argue that issues of such importance would be ignored and the decision for war made on the basis of whether our first-term forces were entirely voluntary or mixed.

As discussed earlier in this report, an all-volunteer military is not expected to differ significantly from the present mixed force in its size, composition, and relations with civilian society. Its subordination to the nation's political leaders will change not at all. The belief that volunteers will be more aggressive, will have greater autonomy from the civilian leadership, and will exploit international tensions to their own advantage springs, not from any rational evidence, but from an irrational fear of relying on the neglected mechanism of freedom to preserve and protect our nation.

CHAPTER 13

Conscription in America

Throughout our nation's history, state and federal governments have compelled service to meet emergencies. Nevertheless, a permanent and comprehensive peacetime draft, such as we have known since 1948, is a recent departure.

During the colonial period, hundreds of conscription laws dealt with specific requirements for service, provided exemptions and penalties, and laid down procedures. Induction into the local militia generally entailed the obligations that are imposed on a reservist today. A militiaman was required to attend drills and was available for call-up to repel Indian attacks or invaders. The maximum term of active service was usually three months, and in some instances the militia could not be used beyond the borders of its colony. Despite the existence of such draft laws, colonial militias were primarily made up of volunteers.

The colonies were opposed to the idea of a common defense establishment. Memories were still fresh of oppressive acts by standing armies under Cromwell, Charles II, and James II of England. The colonists' fear that a large standing army might result in loss of religious and political freedom denied General Washington access to a centralized and compulsory system of procuring men and supplies. Hence, the War of Independence was fought almost entirely by volunteers who were attracted by bounties either to the state militia or the Continental Army. To the limited extent that state militias resorted to the draft, its effect was mitigated by the exemptions available to men who were married, who paid a commutation fee, or who offered a substitute. The militia draft was more a means of taxation than of compulsory procurement of manpower.

Setting a pattern of rapid post-war demobilization which has recurred throughout our history until World War II, the Continental Congress reduced the standing army almost literally to a corporal's guard—some 80 men—soon after the War of Independence. Such weakness left the Confederation unable to suppress Shays' Rebellion and protect against the continued threat of foreign invasion and Indian attacks. To remedy the defects of the Confederation, the Constitutional Convention was called in 1787.

The new Constitution was ultimately a compromise between two fears: (1) that the federal government would remain too weak to maintain order or prevent invasion, and (2) that the federal government might misuse its newly granted power to curb the rights and relative independence of the former colonies. In the field of military affairs, the compromise took the form of balancing the independence of state militias against the need for both a standing army and some centralized control over the state militias. The Constitution gave the federal government the powers to tax, to raise and maintain an army and navy, and to declare war. The states retained the right to raise the militia, to appoint its officers, and to supervise its training in accordance with federal directives. The Constitution explicitly provided that the militia could be placed under federal control only to "execute the Laws of the Union, Suppress Insurrections and repel Invasions." And the Second Amendment identified the state militia as a bulwark of freedom.

In 1790 Congress rejected Secretary of War Knox's proposal for a combination of universal militia service and a federal draft. The question of conscription next arose during the War of 1812. After war was declared, President Madison and Congress approved creation of a 166,000-man army composed primarily of militiamen. However, three New England states were opposed to the war and refused to conscript militia forces. In addition, the regular army had difficulty recruiting. As a result, the armed forces never reached the desired size and sustained an almost unbroken series of defeats, culminating in the burning of the nation's capital in 1814.

To reverse this tide of events, the President requested that Congress conscript 40,000 men. The proposal was fiercely debated. Finally, both the Senate and the House passed bills that would have instituted a modified draft. Before the houses of Congress could resolve their differences, however, the war had ended.

The threat of conscription had created a real danger that New England would secede from the Union. Interestingly, the draft contemplated by both the Senate and the House was more a recruiting vehicle than a comprehensive system of conscription. Both the House and Senate bills divided the population either by state or nationwide into groups, each representing a cross-section of socioeconomic classes. Each group would be compelled either to provide money or "volunteers." The volunteer would be induced to serve by a bounty raised among that group, or, if necessary, would be selected from among its members. Thus both the House and the Senate bills explicitly recognized that everyone should be taxed according to his ability to pay in order to compensate the men who actually did serve.

Once again, the end of the War of 1812 saw a rapid decrease in the size of the standing army. After 1815, a small army was maintained until 1846 and the outbreak of the Mexican War. Although it lasted more than two years, neither conscripts nor the state militia were used to fight this war.

The Civil War, the greatest conflict ever waged on this continent, was largely fought by volunteers on both sides. When war was declared, the Union Army had fewer than 16,000 officers and men. Within the first two years, more than one million men answered the call to arms. Nevertheless, President Lincoln proposed a national draft in early 1863 to ensure that the necessary troops would be forthcoming. When it was enacted in March, the draft immediately aroused widespread resistance, which reached a bloody climax in the New York draft riots. The street fighting left more than 1,000 dead.

Like the draft proposed during the War of 1812, the Civil War draft was not a "pure" system of conscription.

A draftee could provide a substitute or initially purchase an exemption for $300. Although conscription accounted for about 250,000 of the 2,667,000 men who served in the Union Army, only some 46,000 were actually drafted into personal service. Of the balance of those subject to the draft, almost 87,000 purchased an exemption and more than 116,000 provided substitutes. True draftees accounted for only 2.3 percent of the military manpower raised by the North.

In theory, the South had universal conscription. Because of a wide range of exemptions, however, only 170,000 men were conscripts out of the 1.2 million who served in the Confederate Army.

In the South and the North alike, therefore, the draft was not a true system of conscription or a comprehensive system of military manpower recruitment. Even so, the unpopularity of the draft was apparent not only in the riots it touched off but also in the widespread and disruptive draft resistance which caused the suspension of *habeas corpus* in many areas. Surprisingly, the constitutionality of the 1863 Conscription Act was never tested in the federal courts. One fairly obvious reason was the suspension of *habeas corpus,* which eliminated the primary means of raising the constitutionality issue.

Still, there was an important state case—*Kneedler v. Lane*—in which a divided Pennsylvania court upheld the constitutionality of the 1863 Conscription Act. The court held that the draft represented a valid recognition of, on the one hand, the Government's need to be able to wage a war and, on the other, the individual citizen's obligation to serve his country.

Kneedler v. Lane was the first case upholding the constitutionality of a wartime federal draft. The constitutional question was not reconsidered until World War I. (In the meantime, the United States used only volunteers to fight the brief war against Spain in 1898.) In 1917, a comprehensive draft law was passed immediately after the declaration of war and precluded primary reliance on volunteers. Men were drafted into federalized National Guard units and the constitutional distinction between the army and the militia virtually disappeared.

All enlistments were forbidden in 1918 so as not to

upset "the orderly process of selection" established by the preceding year's Act. Basically it evaluated the contribution of each registrant to the war effort and made the least "valuable" the most eligible. The effect of this procedure was certainly inequitable. It meant that, as in the Civil War, the poor inevitably bore a disproportionate share of the burden of service. For example, Negroes represented 13 percent of those inducted although they accounted for only 9.6 percent of total registrants. Another unique aspect of the draft was its effect on military pay. In the past, military pay had risen during a war and had always exceeded comparable manufacturing earnings. In World War I, almost total reliance on the draft relieved Congress of the necessity for providing pay increases or enlistment bonuses, even though the cost of living rose during the war. For the first time, a soldier's pay was less than that of his civilian counterpart.

Opposition to the 1917 Act was less violent than the response to the Civil War draft even though this was the first measure that conscripted men for foreign service. Evasion replaced open resistance, and more than 250,000 draftees failed to appear for induction.

In contrast to the Civil War experience, the constitutionality of the 1917 Selective Draft Law was immediately challenged in the federal courts. A number of cases were consolidated by the Supreme Court and decided unanimously in the *Selective Draft Law Cases*. The significance of this case has been magnified over time because the Supreme Court has never again formally reconsidered the draft's constitutionality.

The Court upheld the law, citing as the only precedents *Kneedler v. Lane* and several Confederate cases. The Court noted that the Constitution granted Congress the power to "raise and support armies"; "to declare wars"; and "to make all laws which shall be necessary and proper for carrying into execution the foregoing powers." The Court argued that these powers would be rendered ineffectual if any limit were imposed upon their use. On that theory Congress had the power to conscript men for war or any other legitimate purpose.

The *Selective Draft Law Cases* hold that the effective exercise of the war power may require a wartime draft.

After World War I the draft expired and the nation again seemed content with a small standing army. Meanwhile, however, the National Guard was brought into closer association with the Regular Army through an amendment to the 1916 National Defense Act. By that amendment, enacted in 1933, units which met federal standards were paid by the Federal Government and redesignated as units of the National Guard of the United States. Thus, distinctions carefully drawn in the Constitution were first blurred by Civil War conscription, then nearly eradicated in World War I, and finally made to disappear completely in 1933. Only those units not up to federal standards would retain the status of a separate state militia.

In 1940, with war in progress in Europe, Congress passed a draft law on September 14, 1940. The constitutionality of this new law was at once challenged. Relying almost entirely on the *Selective Draft Law Cases,* district courts in four major cases rejected the argument that a peacetime draft was unconstitutional. Essentially, the courts reasoned that it was unrealistic to construe the Constitution and the *Selective Draft Law Cases* to mean that an actual war must be declared before a draft could be instituted. They pointed out that military technology permitted the launching of massive surprise attacks with devastating effect and concluded that it was essential for the nation to be able to prepare adequately for war, as well as to wage it. On the grounds that military necessity required a broader construction of Congress' power under the Constitution, the district courts decided that the power to raise armies by conscription was no longer dependent upon the power to declare war.

Legal challenges and general opposition to the draft virtually ceased when Pearl Harbor plunged the United States into war. As in World War I, the draft was the principal source of military manpower, inducing many men to enlist and providing directly more than 10 million, or 61 percent, of the 16.5 million men who donned uniforms.

The draft again enabled the Government to keep military pay at levels significantly lower than comparable civilian pay. The World War II Selective Service System established a structure of deferments and exemptions which has remained relatively unchanged down to the present day. The World War II draft was the first genuinely popular system of conscription.

The draft law was allowed to expire on March 31, 1947, as part of the rapid demobilization typical of the nation's behavior in postwar periods. The military soon expressed concern that it would not be able to obtain the necessary number of volunteers which might, in part, have reflected a 23 percent decrease in the Army's recruiting budget. Simultaneously, President Truman was vigorously promoting universal military training, which Congress rejected in June, 1948. Instead, Congress passed a draft act which was extended for short periods until the Korean War. In January, 1949, the Army ended the two-year enlistment, raised standards higher, and refused to accept volunteers with dependents. Nevertheless, young men continued to enlist. Only 30,000 men were inducted during the period from June, 1948, until the outbreak of the Korean War.

During the Korean War itself the draft provided 27 percent of those in uniform. The Korean War caused Congress to extend the 1948 draft law; and in 1951 it continued the draft authority for a four-year period. This four-year enactment completed the evolution of the draft into a permanent part of the military manpower procurement structure, even though the nation was not fighting either a major or a declared war.

Until the United States' commitment in Vietnam rose sharply in 1965, the draft seemed to be generally accepted as a necessary means of military manpower procurement. There was virtually no debate or opposition to the extension of the Universal Military Service and Training Act in 1955, 1959, and 1963. This was not too surprising. Following the Korean War, military force levels decreased and the impact of the draft declined while the number of draft age youth increased.

During the early 1960's, 95 percent of those between the ages of 18 and 35 were excluded from the I-A and I-A-O pool. The Selective Service System found itself faced with the problem of allocating an excess supply of eligible youth. Its solution was to create new deferments or expand the scope of existing ones. In addition, induction standards were raised and rejection rates increased during the early 1960's. Meanwhile, pay for first-term enlisted men remained below civilian levels. Even so, young men continued to volunteer and the draft call-ups remained relatively small. By 1964-65 only 5,000-10,000 men were being inducted each month, and the average age of induction was almost 23.

The escalation of the Vietnam War in 1965 once again focused attention on the draft. Monthly calls rose sharply to 20,000-30,000. Deferment criteria were tightened, and the average age of inductees declined to 19. Of the 6 million men who have served in the Armed Forces during the Vietnam War, 25 percent have been draftees. In the past few years numerous articles and books have been written about the draft and both a Congressional panel and a Presidential commission have been created to study the Selective Service System. The Marshall Commission, appointed by President Johnson in 1966, published an extensive analysis of how the draft works and concluded that the primary age of draft liability should be 19. The Marshall Commission also urged a random system of selection similar to the one that has since been adopted.

Both before and during the Korean War, there were cases in which inductees questioned the draft's legality. In general, the federal courts either refused to reconsider the constitutionality question or explicitly upheld peacetime conscription as a legitimate and necessary measure to maintain readiness for war. They usually took judicial notice of the threatening international situation which has characterized the cold war period and noted the need for a high degree of military preparedness.

The Supreme Court has increasingly treated the constitutional question as settled. Although the issue has not been directly reconsidered, the Supreme Court has commented in passing on the draft's constitutionality. In a 1953 case the Court said that the draft was a valid exercise of the war power and must function in times of peril as well as during declared wars. In 1968 the Supreme Court said in *U.S. v. O'Brien:*

"The Constitutional power of Congress to raise and support armies and to make all laws necessary and proper to that end is broad and sweeping . . . The power of Congress to classify and conscript manpower for military service is beyond question."

The only citation in support of this firm conclusion was the *Selective Draft Law Cases* which dealt with a *wartime* draft.

The Founding Fathers feared conscription by the central government would lead to unnecessary abridgment of personal freedoms. Until the Civil War there was no draft; the system of compulsory service instituted in 1863 was born of necessity and was, in any event, far short of being comprehensive. In both 1917 and 1940 the draft emerged again as a wartime expedient. In 1948 the Selective Service System was revived to maintain preparedness for cold war crises. After the Korean War, it remained in existence and was once again an important source of manpower when the nation became deeply involved in Vietnam in 1965. Given the nation's legal and political traditions, the relatively recent phenomenon of a continuing peacetime draft should be re-evaluated.

CHAPTER 14

Recent Foreign Experience
with Voluntarism

Great Britain, Canada, and, until 1965, Australia have all manned their armed forces on a completely voluntary basis in the recent past. Because the United States shares with these countries a common cultural heritage, we have examined their experiences with all-volunteer forces to anticipate problems which might arise once the draft was ended in the United States. Of course, due allowance must be made for differences as well as similarities in evaluating the impact of ending the draft in other societies.

The British experience is most helpful because they maintain relatively larger forces than the other two countries. Also their comparatively recent decision to abandon conscription sheds light on the transition process as well as the steady state experience.

Britain's decision in 1957 to end conscription coincided with a new defense policy emphasizing nuclear deterrence, withdrawal from positions east of Suez, and a cutback in force levels to 400,000 from 700,000. By 1960 the transition was virtually completed, and all inductions ceased.

The elimination of conscription increased the average length of service per man by approximately 200 percent, from less than three years under the draft to roughly eight. While this increase reflects in part use of long initial terms of service (6 or 9 years) it also shows that true volunteers were more likely to stay in the service than conscripts.

Another important effect of ending conscription was the decline in the proportion of troops in training from 21 percent to 14 percent despite an increase in the average length of training per man. Thus, an all-volunteer force has enabled the British to maintain a higher proportion of troops in an effective status.

British officials have said that the fully volunteer force is more productive than a mixed force because of lower turnover and the superior performance of more experienced servicemen. A precise measure of this improved productivity is not possible, but the British are able to assess any changes in the quality of their armed forces by such measures as educational attainment and aptitude scores. These show that the Royal Navy and Air Force have experienced no decline in quality since conscription ended, and that the quality of Army recruits has slipped slightly—the proportion of volunteers falling in the lowest 30 percent aptitude category increasing by perhaps 2 percent. Some British Army officers assert that improved motivation and morale in the enlisted ranks since the end of conscription far outweigh the loss of a relatively small number of high quality draftees.

During the past several years the British have experienced a decline in enlistments which is beginning to threaten the achievement of target force levels. There appear to be four reasons for this shortfall. First, more young men are staying in school. Second, new government policies expanding the availability of both apprentice and advanced training have made civilian employment relatively more attractive to youth. The latter factor is especially important in Britain because 15–17-year-olds enlist primarily to get training. Third, British youths are less willing to undertake long initial minimum tours of duty ranging from five to twelve years. Fourth, there has been a decline in the number of youths aged 16 to 24 in the population.

To increase enlistments, the British Army introduced in April, 1969 a shorter minimum enlistment of three years. The initial response has been good and this shorter option has not significantly reduced the number enlisting for longer terms. Thus, relatively short-term enlistments, perhaps supplemented by pay increases, could provide an adequate number of British recruits in the foreseeable future.

Conscription in Australia ceased after World War II. During the Korean War a system of Universal Military Training was introduced requiring every qualified male to complete three months of training and then serve in the Australian reserves. The active duty forces never used these conscripts and only volunteers fought in Korea and Malaya. This system ceased in 1958 and the Australian forces were manned exclusively by volunteers. But, in October of 1964, the Australian government decided to raise force levels from 49,000 to 76,000 by instituting a draft by lottery.

Some have cited the Australian decision to return to a draft as evidence that an all-volunteer force is not feasible for the United States. There are several reasons why this argument by analogy is inappropriate. First, the Australians have not made a concerted effort to attract additional recruits on a voluntary basis. Once the decision was made to use conscription to raise force levels, no serious effort was made to increase voluntary enlistments either by raising pay or redoubling recruiting efforts. Second, the Australian economy is heavily unionized and apprenticeship programs requiring four or more years deplete the pool of men available for military service. Third, Australia has enjoyed a rapid growth in its economy (the unemployment rate is about 1 percent) which makes civilian jobs relatively more attractive than military service. Finally, civilian earnings significantly exceed military pay rates. Civilians receive overtime and other supplementary compensation in excess of the common wage rates set by the government for both the military and the civilian economy.

The Australians could have expanded the size of the Armed Forces on a voluntary basis by raising pay and reorganizing recruiting. Given the important differences between the two countries, one cannot conclude that the Australian experience shows that the United States would be unable to attract enough recruits on a voluntary basis if energetic and efficient recruiting were combined with competitive rates of pay.

The Canadian Armed Forces have always been entirely voluntary except for the period from 1940 to early 1945. The Canadian forces presently number slightly less than 100,000 men, supported by an annual inflow of about 12,000 men. The quality of the entrants is remarkably high; almost all fall within the upper half of the population as measured by mental aptitude. Military pay more nearly approximates civilian earnings—the monthly pay for privates is $225. Attracting recruits has posed no problem in Canada, and recruiting officers suggest that the number of enlistments could be doubled or tripled with no difficulty.

The Canadian armed force is relatively small; it is roughly equivalent, on a population basis, to an American force of one million men. However, budgetary constraints rather than recruiting difficulties are responsible for the size of Canada's forces.

The recent experiences of the British, Australian, and Canadian Armed Forces suggest that competitive wages will attract an adequate quantity and quality of volunteers. There is no evidence in any of these countries that all-volunteer forces are alienated from the rest of society.

CHAPTER 15

Alternatives
to an All-Volunteer Force

What are the alternatives both to the present system of conscription and to an all-volunteer armed force? In this chapter the Commission weighs various suggestions which have been raised.

One proposed alternative is National Service. Many National Service proposals involve purely voluntary service. Such proposals are actually supplements, rather than alternatives, to an all-volunteer armed force. Other proposals would require service on the part of all those eligible. In our analysis of alternatives to an all-volunteer force, we have considered only the mandatory proposals. While these mandatory National Service proposals differ in detail, they would generally require service of all youth, though not necessarily in the military. Most would permit individuals to choose how they would serve from among a limited set of alternatives.

Advocates of National Service have suggested a variety of approaches. Some have urged that literally everyone, male and female, be required to serve, even those who are physically or mentally disabled or morally unfit. Because of the high cost of formal and on-the-job training, National Service on a one-year basis would be prohibitively expensive. National Service for two years would mean employing almost 8,000,000 young people, or 4,000,000 if females are excluded. If longer terms of service were instituted for more attractive types of duty, these numbers would be even larger. Assuming a very modest annual cost for each participant of $4,000 to $5,000, the cost of such a program would be a minimum of $16 billion, and perhaps as much as $40 billion—an amount equal to the entire current manpower budget of the Department of Defense. In short, the numbers of men and cost of mandatory National Service are staggering.

Advocates of other proposals argue that some individuals should be excused from serving. If that were the case, deferments and exemptions would proliferate just as they have under the draft. A new Selective Service System would be required to administer a non-universal National Service program.

Regardless of the administrative procedure used, a National Service program would not be able to prevent glaring inequities among those who served. Not all National Service would be equally desirable (or repugnant), and those with higher qualifications would probably find their way into the more desirable positions. If this inequity were minimized by introducing a system of differential terms of service, the ranks of those engaged in National Service and its cost would increase further.

The appeal of mandatory National Service, in large measure, arises from the manifest inequities in the present system of conscription. It promises to eliminate these inequities by forcing a larger proportion of the populace to serve in some capacity—and hence to pay a tax-in-kind. In practice it not only perpetuates such an inequitable tax, but extends it to a larger segment of the population. The cure for inequity is not its extension.

Above all, mandatory National Service is coercive and involuntary. Such a system of universal conscription would require all those eligible to serve within a specified period of time. If insufficient numbers proved willing to enlist in the military or volunteer for other onerous types of government service, some would be compelled to serve in these less desirable capacities. In essence, mandatory National Service requires forced labor. Although motivated by a genuine interest in the nation's welfare, advocates of mandatory National Service are suggesting a compulsory system which is more consistent with a totalitarian than a democratic heritage. If the service that youth would render is important and valuable enough to merit public support, it can and should be financed through general taxation like other government programs.

Universal Military Training resembles mandatory National Service, for it contemplates conscription of all those eligible. It is undesirable for generally the same reasons as mandatory National Service. For one thing, it would impose on the military more untrained personnel than can be productively employed. A one-year tour of duty—the usual term proposed—is prohibitively expensive in view of the very short period an individual would serve after receiving costly training. Assuming current eligibility standards, a two-year tour would force on the services more than 2,000,000 non-career persons at any given time. Whether or not UMT is unconstitutional, it would definitely represent a sharp break with the nation's traditional respect for individual freedom.

The lottery draft recently adopted is at best an expedient. It is important to recognize that the tax inequity implicit in the draft is not eliminated by substituting a lottery for present methods of selection. In theory, the lottery makes it equally probable that any individual might be selected from those eligible to serve. It thus aims at equity in selection. But equity in selection is not equity in service. Those few who are selected to serve, whether at random or otherwise, still pay a large tax-in-kind in order to reduce taxes for the majority. Moreover, it is by no means clear that the lottery achieves greater equity even in selection. No doubt one can find many instances of inequitable treatment of draftees under Selective Service. Even so, it does not logically follow that the system as a whole is more unjust than a random system. Many local draft boards and some of the general rules for deferments and exemptions actually do more to achieve equity than the system of random selection. Local boards can and do take into account an individual's particular circumstances.

The lottery reduces the number of draft induced volunteers and thereby necessitates an increase in the number of draftees. Because draftees serve two-year terms and volunteers three, personnel turnover and the attendant costs are increased.

The lottery offers one advantage over Selective Service. When it is combined with the proposal to expose potential draftees to a one-time jeopardy at age 19, it reduces the uncertainty confronting an individual about whether he will be required to serve, and thereby mitigates the distortion in career and personal planning endured under Selective Service.

APPENDICES

Budget Expenditures
for All-Volunteer Forces

This appendix describes the methods and assumptions employed to derive estimated budgets for all-volunteer and mixed forces of equal effective strengths. The mixed forces examined employ a 19-year-old lottery as the means of selecting draftees. Limitations of space preclude an exhaustive analysis of estimation procedures. These detailed analyses will be reported in a forthcoming volume containing background studies.

Supply of Enlisted Personnel

In our analyses of mixed forces we have assumed that only the Army will have to conscript men, and then only for its enlisted ranks. Sufficient reservists, officers, and enlisted men for the other services were presumed to be available on a "voluntary" basis, even though some of them will be draft-motivated. These assumptions are consistent with recent experience.

Procedurally, monthly draft calls are determined as a residual; they are the difference between requirements for Army recruits and the number of Regular Army enlistments. Given requirements, draft calls will be negatively related to enlistments; the higher the enlistments, the smaller the draft calls. If one looks at the data, however, he will find that draft calls have been positively related to enlistments. Higher draft calls have been accompanied by increased enlistments, because many poten-

TABLE A–I.—Voluntary enlistments and Army inductions by service

	Regular Army enlistments	Army inductions	Navy	Marine Corps	Air Force	Dept. of Defense [1]
Number of voluntary enlistments, annual average FY 1963–65 (000)						
Mental groups I–III	95.3	73.3	76.3	29.1	81.5	282.2
Mental group IV	7.3	35.9	8.7	1.8	5.9	23.8
All mental groups	102.6	109.2	85.0	30.9	87.4	305.9
Voluntary enlistment rates under Selective Service draft: FY 1963–65 [2]						
Mental groups I–III	1.56	1.20	1.25	0.48	1.33	4.62
Mental group IV	0.12	0.59	0.14	0.03	0.10	0.39
All mental groups	1.68	1.79	1.39	0.51	1.43	5.01
Percentage of true volunteers (k)	56.6	12.3	63.4	69.9	56.6	59.8
True voluntary enlistment rates in the absence of a draft						
Mental groups I–III	1.03	—	0.79	0.33	0.75	2.91
All mental groups	1.29	—	0.99	0.42	0.94	3.63
Number of true enlistments, annual averages FY 1977–79 [3]						
Mental groups I–III	88.3	—	67.9	28.6	64.8	249.6
Mental group IV	22.1	—	17.0	7.1	16.2	62.4
All mental groups	110.4	—	84.9	35.7	81.0	312.0

[1] Excludes data for Army inductions.
[2] Enlistment rates are expressed as a percentage of 17–20-year-old male population for the annual average 1963–65.
[3] The 17–20-year-old male population is projected to average 8,589 thousand in FY 1977–79.

tial draftees prefer the advantages of enlisting to the prospect of being an inductee. When requirements rise, the probability of being drafted rises and induces an increase in draft-motivated enlistments. Our projections for the mixed forces incorporate this type of supply response. Army enlistments rise by 235 men per year in response to an increase in draft calls of 1,000 individuals. By shortening the period of draft liability, the 19-year-old lottery now in effect will tend to reduce the flow of draft-motivated volunteers relative to calls (independently of the response to varying levels of draft calls). In our projections the voluntary enlistment rates experienced under Selective Service have been reduced by 12.5 percent to provide for the effect of the 19-year-old lottery.

The average annual flow of voluntary enlistments under the former Selective Service draft for the period FY 1963-65 is shown at the top of table A-I. During this period, mental group IV annual accessions (men with mental test scores between the 10th and 30th percentiles) were controlled by the services and limited to a total of about 15 percent of enlistments and inductions. Voluntary enlistments and Army inductions of men in mental groups I-III are expressed as percentages of the 17–20-year-old male population on line 4 of table A-I. These are enlistment and induction rates.

The "voluntary" enlistments in FY 1963 through 1965 included many draft-motivated volunteers who indicated in the 1964 Department of Defense survey that if there had been no draft they would *not* have volunteered for active military service. Moreover, the inductees included some who said they were also true volunteers, i.e., they would have enlisted in the absence of a draft. The percentage of true volunteers (line 7 of table A-I) represents the percentage of first-term enlisted men who stated in the 1964 survey that they probably or definitely would have volunteered in the absence of a draft. By multiplying lines 4 and 7, we arrive at the estimated true volunteer enlistment rate of men in mental groups I through III (line 8), assuming that the draft is abolished with no change in the ratio of military to civilian pay.

For our projections we assumed that each service would accept up to a *maximum* of 20 percent mental group IV

TABLE A-II.—Annual compensation of military personnel, by service [1]
[in constant 1969 prices]

Component	Army	Navy	Marine Corps	Air Force	Department of Defense
First-term enlisted men					
Current pay M_0	$3,686	$3,687	$3,320	$3,746	$3,812
Proposed pay M_1 [2]	5,081	4,942	4,573	5,003	5,066
Ratio M_1/M_0	1.378	1.340	1.377	1.336	1.328
Second-term enlisted men					
Current Pay M_0	8,179	8,838	8,097	8,596	8,605
Proposed pay M_1	8,816	9,193	8,548	9,071	9,071
Ratio M_1/M_0	1.078	1.040	1.056	1.055	1.054
First-term officers					
Current Pay M_0	8,103	8,270	8,316	8,493	8,595
Proposed pay M_1	9,693	9,539	9,575	9,764	9,854
Ratio M_1/M_0	1.196	1.153	1.151	1.150	1.146

[1] The annual compensation of first-term enlisted men and officers is a weighted average of regular military compensation (defined in ch. 5) over the first term consisting of 3 years for Army enlisted men and 4 years for enlisted men in other Services and for all officers. Annual compensation of second-term enlisted men is a weighted average of total compensation over the 4 years of the second term. The weights are based on a discount rate of 10 percent per year.

[2] The compensation figures for all four services are based on the same pay table. Differences in average compensation levels among the services are due to differences in the distribution by length of service.

TABLE A–III.—Voluntary enlistment rates and sustainable force strength in the absence of a draft [in thousands]

	Army	Navy	Marine Corps	Air Force	Department of Defense
True voluntary enlistment rates with					
1. No pay increase E_0	1.285	0.989	0.416	0.943	3.633
2. Recommended pay increase E_0^*	1.919	1.427	.621	1.356	5.323
3. Ratio E_0^*/E_0	1.493	1.443	1.492	1.436	1.465
Sustainable force strength with no pay increase by					
4. FY 1975	620.1	553.9	176.9	558.4	1,909.3
5. FY 1980	649.0	604.4	191.5	571.4	2,016.3
Sustainable force strengths with recommended pay increase by					
6. FY 1975	784.8	690.5	234.4	683.9	2,393.6
7. FY 1980	877.9	798.2	268.3	753.5	2,697.9
Equilibrium all-volunteer enlisted strength objectives					
8. 2.0 million men	624.3	439.0	148.0	471.2	1,682.5
9. 2.25 million men	691.9	487.2	178.6	528.6	1,886.3
10. 2.5 million men	827.1	518.6	184.8	558.9	2,089.4
11. 3.0 million men	1,046.9	625.3	204.8	628.2	2,505.2

enlistments. The fraction of mental group IV enlistments was allowed to fall below the 20 percent maximum whenever the supply of true volunteers exceeded requirements.

The flow of true volunteers, in the absence of a draft and with no pay changes in the period FY 1977-79, was estimated by applying the true voluntary enlistment rates to the projected 17-to-20-year-old male population of 8,589,000 men in this period; this is presented in the bottom panel of table A-I.

Several statistical studies were made to estimate the responsiveness of supplies of voluntary enlistments to changes in the ratio of military to civilian pay. In two time series studies, quarterly data on Army and Air Force enlistment rates were related to the ratio of military to civilian pay, draft pressure, and unemployment. In a third cross-sectional study, regional differences in enlistment rates were related to differences in civilian pay and unemployment. In these studies, the unemployment variable was insignificant, and was thus ignored in our projections. The elasticity of supply (defined as the percentage change in voluntary enlistments resulting from a given percentage change in military pay) which was estimated in these studies, ranged from 1 to 2.2; i.e., a one percent increase in military pay can be expected to raise voluntary enlistments by 1 to 2.2 percent.

The pay recommendations reported in chapter 5 of this volume would produce the pay levels for first-term enlisted men shown in the top panel of table A-II. An elasticity of $+1.25$ (which is on the low end of the range found in our studies) was used to estimate the effect of this pay increase on the supply of voluntary enlistments in the absence of a draft. The true voluntary enlistment rates with no pay increase E_0 and with the higher recommended pay rates E_0^* are shown in the first two lines of table A-III.

If the draft were ended in FY 1971 with no changes in military pay (i.e. enlistment rates E_0 apply), the flow of true volunteers would sustain the enlisted active duty force strengths shown in lines 4 and 5 of table A-III. The larger flows of volunteers that would be attracted by the higher recommended pay levels could support the larger

active duty forces shown in lines 6 and 7. For comparative purposes, the four equilibrium all-volunteer forces
are presented in the bottom panel of table A-III. Given
the recommended pay increase, the sustainable all-volunteer forces attain levels by FY 1980 that are above the
target levels for the 2.0, 2.25, and 2.5 million man forces.
Indeed, a 2.0 million man force could be raised with no
pay change provided true volunteers exhibit the projected
higher re-enlistment rates of the model. It should be em-
phasized that these conclusions pertain to the force in
existence in 1980, and not to the force strengths in the
intervening years. In order to maintain a force of 2.0
million men during the transition years FY 1973 to 1976,
some modest pay increases would be needed.

The number of accessions required to meet any given
force strength objective is a function of losses of active
duty personnel. Men are separated from the Armed Forces
for various reasons such as medical disability, unsuitable
performance, hardship, retirement, and most importantly,
failure to re-enlist after completing an obligated term.
The vast majority of enlisted and officer losses occur at
the end of the first term of service. The loss rates which
would be experienced by an all-volunteer force are expected to be considerably lower than those in a mixed
force. Two-year draftees would be replaced by three-year
regular enlistments. Moreover, Department of Defense
surveys of enlisted men support the conclusion that draft-
motivated volunteers exhibit lower re-enlistment rates than
true volunteers. Finally, the services' experience with
proficiency pay and regular and variable re-enlistment
bonuses has shown that pay increases for the career enlisted force can raise re-enlistment rates. Reference to
table A-II reveals that the recommended pay increase
needed to move to an all-volunteer force would raise the
pay of second-term enlisted men by roughly 7 percent.

The responsiveness of supplies of first-term re-enlistments to military pay changes (referred to above as the
elasticity of supply) was estimated in three studies. All
three studies reported elasticity estimates which ranged
from 2.0 to 4.5; i.e., a 10 percent increase in the pay of
second-term enlisted men results in re-enlistment rates that
are 20 to 45 percent above their previous levels. Again, the

elasticity estimates used in our projections were taken from the lower end of the intervals reported in the three studies (line 2 of table A-IV).

Even if the draft were ended with no pay changes our studies indicate that re-enlistment rates would rise when all recruits voluntarily enter the service. The estimated percentage increase in re-enlistments when the mixed inputs of true and draft-motivated volunteers are replaced by true volunteers is shown in the third line of table A-IV.

TABLE A–IV.—Estimated first-term reenlistment rates in mixed and all-volunteer forces

	Army	Navy	Marine Corps	Air Force
1. Relative increase in second term pay (M_1/M_0)[1]	1.078	1.040	1.056	1.055
2. Elasticity of supply—B ..	2.43	2.14	2.00	2.36
3. Percentage increase due to all-volunteer recruits ..	39	25	20	47
Estimated first-term reenlistment rates				
4. Mixed force continued draft (r_0)	0.175	0.197	0.140	0.184
5. Transition period (r_1) ...	.210	.214	.156	.209
6. All-volunteer force (r_2) ..	.292	.268	.187	.307

[1] The compensated figures for all four services are based on the same pay table. Differences in average compensation levels among the services are due to differences in the distribution by length of service.

The projections of draft calls and required accessions for the mixed forces, assuming a continued lottery draft and no pay changes, were based on loss rates incorporating the re-enlistment rates of line 4. In the move to an all-volunteer force, it was recommended that military pay be increased at the beginning of FY 1971. If the recommended pay raise is implemented on July 1, 1970, the group which receives the largest pay increase (first-term enlisted men) includes a considerable number of draftees and draft-motivated volunteers. It is unlikely, therefore, that first-term re-enlistment rates will immediately climb to their equilibrium levels. Some improvement is anticipated, since the pay raise will make military service more attractive in relation to competing civilian jobs. Hence, for the transition period, we have used the re-enlistment rates shown in line 5. The all-volunteer re-enlistment rates (line 6) reflect both the shift to all-volunteer recruits and the higher pay for enlisted men.

The loss rates used in our projections generate the annual personnel turnover rates for the period FY 1977 through 1979 shown in table A-V. With a draft and with 47 percent of Army accessions projected to be draftees, we estimate that the annual Army enlisted personnel turnover rate will be 27.5 percent. Due to higher retention rates, an all-volunteer Army will have a reduced turnover rate for enlisted men of only 17.9 percent per year. Less striking reductions in turnover are expected to take place in the other services and for officer personnel.

TABLE A–V.—Projected annual turnover rates of mixed and all-volunteer forces *
[for effective strength of 2.5 million men]

Service	Mixed force		All-volunteer force	
	Enlisted	Officers	Enlisted	Officers
Army	27.5	9.9	17.9	8.5
Navy	15.8	11.3	14.4	10.4
Marine Corps	19.2	13.5	17.7	13.3
Air Force	16.8	8.6	15.2	9.5
Department of Defense ...	21.1	10.0	16.4	9.5

* The annual personnel turnover rates are the average annual accessions in FY 1977–79 expressed as a percentage of the average active duty force strength during the period. Data based on projections for a mixed force of 2.5 million men.

Comparing sustainable force strengths to target force levels (table A-III), or comparing required accessions to the flow of true volunteers, confirms the fact that the Army is likely to suffer the largest manpower deficits if the draft is ended. The recruitment problem which confronts an all-volunteer force is an Army problem. This is not surprising since the Army is the only service which has consistently relied on draft calls to meet its manpower requirements.

In estimating the levels of military pay needed to attract the requisite numbers of recruits we have concentrated on Army enlisted manpower deficits. This procedure involves a safe assumption that if the Army's manpower demands can be met, the other services will certainly be able to staff their forces with qualified men. This procedure also tends to overstate the requisite increase in military pay, since it tacitly assumes that excess supplies of enlistment applicants to the other services would *not* spill over into the Army.

Officer Supply

Under conscription, the number of applicants for most officer procurement programs has exceeded requirements. It is anticipated that this situation will prevail even in the absence of a draft for the highly selective programs such as the military academies and ROTC (Reserve Officer Training Corps) scholarships. Other programs such as the non-scholarship ROTC and various college-graduate, officer-candidate schools may, however, experience shortfalls. Because the flow of actual entrants has been less than the number who would have volunteered under a draft, data on actual officer accessions do not provide a satisfactory basis for projecting future supplies.

The supplies of officers to an all-volunteer force depend critically on three factors: (1) the intensity of the Vietnam War, (2) the presence or absence of the draft, and (3) the ratio of military to civilian pay. An econometric model using voluntary ROTC enrollment data was developed to estimate the quantitative effects of these three factors. The voluntary enrollment rate of male freshmen at colleges where ROTC participation is *not* compulsory provides us with a supply variable free of the demand constraints which affect other officer procurement programs. The Army has not limited freshman ROTC enrollments, and hence, the enrollment rates reflect the decisions of youths at these colleges.

The non-scholarship ROTC program has been the major source of Army officers, and the Army will probably have the severest officer recruitment problem in an all-volunteer force. This assumption is plausible since the

Army is the only service which has offered a two-year obligated term (and at one time a six-month term) for newly commissioned officers. The other services have adopted three, four and five year obligated terms even for ROTC officers. The estimated pay increase needed to attract enough Army officers should be sufficient to attract an adequate number of officers to the other services.

Army ROTC freshman enrollment rates exhibited a sharp decline during the last half of the 1960's so that by 1970 they were about half of the rate in 1964. This decline closely correlates with casualty rates in Vietnam.

TABLE A–VI.—Actual and projected proportion of male freshman enrollments in Army ROTC programs in voluntary schools [1]
1960–80

Year	Enrollment rate with a draft		Estimated enrollment rate without draft [3]
	Actual	Estimated [2]	
1960–62	0.196	0.202	0.089
1963–65	.145	.145	.080
1966–68	.159	.156	.075
1969–70	.098	.107	.047
Projected			
1971–73		0.074 [4]	0.041
1974–77		.114	.063
1978–80		.134	.074

[1] In the period of 1960–65, all enrollments were in 4-year ROTC programs. Beginning in 1966, the rates include enrollments in both the 4-year program and estimates of what proportion of additional freshmen would have to volunteer to produce the number of actual enrollments in the 2-year program 2 years hence. The rates also include ROTC scholarship students.

[2] The estimated rates are based on a multivariable regression equation, including as independent variables, relative officer to draftee and civilian earnings, draft probability of college graduates, and the fatality rate of junior Army officers.

[3] Assumes a draft-induced fraction of estimated continued draft enrollments of 56 percent for 1960–62, 1967–70, and 45 percent for 1963–66, 1971–80.

[4] These projections assume that the draft is retained at the prewar (1964) level and the relationship between officer pay and civilian earnings is maintained at the 1970 level.

De-escalation should reverse the trend in FY 1972 and lead to the projected enrollment rates shown in table A-VI. This anticipated reversal in the freshman enrollment rate will, however, have a delayed impact since an increase in the supply of newly commissioned officers will not occur until four years later.

Elimination of the draft will result in a loss of draft-motivated volunteers in Army ROTC programs. Column 2 in table A-VI shows the projected trend in enrollment rates if the draft is continued. The percentage of draft-motivated first-term Army officers who entered through an ROTC program was estimated to be 45 percent in the 1964 Department of Defense survey and 56 percent in the 1968 survey. The lower draft-motivation factor, 45 percent, was employed in projections of Army ROTC officer supplies, on the assumption that pre-Vietnam conditions would prevail during the decade of the 1970's.

The ratio of officer pay to civilian pay of college graduates was found to be a significant variable explaining differences in ROTC enrollment rates. The pay schedules recommended by the Commission will raise the pay of first-term officers by approximately 25 percent (table A-II). Our studies indicate that this pay raise

TABLE A–VII.—Projected Army ROTC enrollment rates

Fiscal Year	Projected enrollment rate—1970 pay scale [1]	Projected enrollment rate— recommended pay scale [2]
1971	.0350	.0448
1972	.0390	.0496
1973	.0480	.0603
1974	.0550	.0687
1975	.0610	.0756
1976	.0650	.0803
1977	.0690	.0852
1978	.0720	.0883
1979	.0740	.0907
1980	.0750	.0917

[1] See ch. 5, table 5-II.
[2] See ch. 5, table 5-III for recommended officer pay table.

should increase the supply of Army ROTC officers by 29 percent. The expected effect of the increased pay on enrollment rates is shown in table A-VII. When the projected voluntary enrollment rates of table A-VII, with the pay increase, are applied to the expanding pool of male college freshmen, the Army meets its officer accession requirements. (The latter statement assumes that the ROTC scholarship program will be expanded as recommended from 5,500 scholarships per service to 10,000 scholarships.)

Additional Budget Expenditures for an All-Volunteer Force

Comparisons of the average budgets required to sustain mixed forces of 2.0, 2.25, 2.5, and 3.0 million men, and to sustain all-volunteer forces with the same effective strengths for FY 1977 through 1979 are given in tables A-VIII, A-IX, A-X, and A-XI. We have chosen the period FY 1977 through 1979 as fairly representing the differences in budget requirements for the mixed and all-volunteer forces. By then, accession requirements will have stabilized, and most of the savings accruing to an all-volunteer force will have taken effect. All of the comparisons are made in constant 1970 dollars, that is, there is no allowance for inflation. The pay profiles used to compute total pay and allowance are those set forth in chapter 5. For all of the mixed forces, we have used estimated pay for FY 1971, which includes an across-the-board increase of 8 percent. For the 2.0, 2.25, and 2.5 million man all-volunteer forces we have used the pay profile recommended by the Commission. The 3.0 million man force requires a further pay increase. In explaining tables A-VIII through A-XI, we have focused on the 2.5 million man force only as an example.

Estimates of the military pay and allowances of enlisted men, officers, and uniformed women (including the imputed value of income-in-kind) for a mixed force of 2.5 million men in the period FY 1977 through 1979, are given at the top of table A-X. Because of lower personnel turnover, an all-volunteer force can have 56.5 thousand less

TABLE A–VIII.—Estimated budget expenditures for mixed and all-volunteer forces FY 1977–1979 [for force of 2.0 million men in billions of 1970 dollars]

	Mixed force	All-volunteer force	Increment
Military pay and allowances:			
Active-duty forces			
1. Enlisted	$11.71	$13.20	$1.49
2. Officers	4.12	4.21	.09
3. Total compensation	15.83	17.41	1.58
Training and turnover related travel costs			
4. Enlisted	.84	.69	—.15
5. Officers	.30	.29	—.01
6. Total training and travel costs	1.14	.98	—.16
Reserve forces			
7. Military pay/allowances	.71	.83	.12
8. Training and travel costs	.24	.25	.01
9. Total reserve forces ...	.95	1.08	.13
Other budget increments			
10. Medical personnel	—	.13	.13
11. Recruiting, ROTC and misc.	—	.08	.08
12. Total other items	—	.21	.21
13. Total	17.92	19.68	1.76
14. Less added Federal income taxes			—.29
15. Net budgetary increase .			1.47

men than a mixed force of 2.5 million and still provide the same effective strength. In spite of this reduction in size, which considered alone reduces budget requirements by $678 million, the military pay and allowances budget for an all-volunteer force is higher than that for the equivalent mixed force for two reasons. First, annual pay rates are higher—especially in the first four years of service. Second, the greater retention of an all-volunteer force means the force is more experienced; hence a larger

TABLE A–IX.—Estimated budget expenditures for mixed and all-volunteer forces FY 1977–79 [for force of 2.25 million men in billions of 1970 dollars]

	Mixed force	All-volunteer force	Increment
Military pay and allowances:			
Active-duty forces			
1. Enlisted			
2. Officers			
3. Total compensation ...	$12.70	$14.46	$1.76
Training and turnover-related	4.54	4.64	.10
travel costs	17.24	19.10	1.86
4. Enlisted			
5. Officers			
6. Total training and	1.02	.84	—.18
travel costs	.36	.35	—.01
Reserve forces	1.38	1.19	—.19
7. Military pay/allowances			
8. Training and travel costs	.79	.93	.14
9. Total reserve forces ...	.24	.27	.03
Other budget increments	1.03	1.20	.17
10. Medical personnel			
11. Recruiting, ROTC	—	.16	.16
and misc.	—	.08	.08
12. Total other items	—	.24	.24
13. Total	19.65	21.73	2.08
14. Less added Federal income taxes			—.34
15. Net budgetary increase ..			1.74

fraction of the men are receiving higher pay rates. Only 38.0 percent of the mixed force is projected to have more than four years of service as compared to 44.6 percent for the all-volunteer force. We estimate that the pay and allowances budget for an all-volunteer force during FY 1977 through 1979 will on average be $2.2 billion higher than would be required for an equally effective mixed force of 2.5 million men.

Although the move to an all-volunteer force entails a

higher military pay and allowances budget, the training and transient budgets, which are largely determined by the flow of new accessions, will fall. Each enlisted recruit receives about one-half of a year of basic military and technical training. The size of the training command can be reduced with the move to a voluntary force because fewer accessions are required to sustain the all-volunteer force. The manpower savings and resulting reduction in the military pay and allowances budget have already been

TABLE A–X.—Estimated budget expenditures for mixed and all-volunteer forces FY 1977–1979
[for force of 2.5 million men in billions of 1970 dollars]

	Mixed force	All-volunteer force	Increment
Military pay and allowances:			
Active-duty forces			
1. Enlisted	$13.67	$15.78	$2.11
2. Officers	5.02	5.15	.13
3. Total compensation ...	18.69	20.93	2.24
Training and turnover related travel costs			
4. Enlisted	1.25	.95	—.30
5. Officers	.41	.39	—.02
6. Total training and travel costs	1.66	1.34	—.32
Reserve forces			
7. Military pay/allowances	.86	1.03	.17
8. Training and travel costs	.22	.29	.07
9. Total reserve forces ...	1.08	1.32	.24
Other budget increments			
10. Proficiency pay (first-term enlisted men) ..	—	.14	.14
11. Medical personnel	—	.16	.16
12. Miscellaneous	—	.08	.08
13. Total other items	—	.38	.38
14. Total	21.43	23.97	2.54
15. Less added Federal income taxes			—.42
16. Net budgetary increase .			2.12

incorporated into the analysis by the reduction of 56,500 men in the all-volunteer force of 2.5 million men. In addition to manpower costs, substantial budget outlays are also needed to finance the material and capital costs of the training command. It was estimated in our study that the material and variable costs over and above the personnel costs of enlisted men are about $2,500 per recruit.

TABLE A–XI.—Estimated budget expenditures for mixed and all-volunteer forces FY 1977–1979
[for force of 3.0 million men in billions of 1970 dollars]

	Mixed force	All-volunteer force	Increment
Military pay and allowances:			
Active-duty forces			
1. Enlisted			
2. Officers			
3. Total compensation ...	$15.79	$20.41	$4.62
Training and turnover related	5.57	6.04	.47
travel costs	21.36	26.45	5.09
4. Enlisted			
5. Officers			
6. Total training and	1.64	1.16	—.47
travel costs	.48	.46	—.03
Reserve forces	2.12	1.62	—.50
7. Military pay/allowances			
8. Training and travel costs	.90	1.19	.29
9. Total reserve forces ...	.13	.28	.15
Other budget increments..	1.03	1.47	.44
10. Proficiency pay (first-term enlisted men) ..			
11. Medical personnel	—	.21	.21
12. Miscellaneous *	—	.20	.20
13. Total other items	—	.08	.08
14. Total ½..............	—	.49	.49
15. Less added Federal	24.51	30.03	5.52
income taxes			—.97
16. Net budgetary increase .			4.55

* Includes $27 million for additional ROTC scholarships and $53 million for additional recruiting expenditures.

Approximately 25,000 positions in the 2.5 million man mixed force must be set aside to accommodate the accession, training, and separation moves of enlisted men. With its lower personnel turnover, an all-volunteer force can economize on the number of positions needed to accomplish these moves, in addition to generating savings in direct travel costs. The direct travel costs per recruit that were paid in 1968 are estimated to be $268. The travel costs per officer accession are even higher—$1,150—because the typical officer is married and must move dependents as well as household belongings. At a force level of 2.5 million men, it is estimated that savings in direct travel costs will average $70 million in FY 1977 through 1979.

The cost of training officers varies widely among different officer procurement programs. It runs as high as $50,000 for an officer trained at the military academies, and is approximately $12,000 for officers commissioned through officer candidate schools. Flight training is an even more expensive proposition, and Department of Defense estimates range from around $50,000 for helicopter pilots to $250,000 for jet fighter pilots. In our projections, it was assumed that the number of officers commissioned through the academies and ROTC scholarship programs would be the same in both the mixed and all-volunteer forces. The college and non-college graduate officer candidate schools have historically been the sources which equilibrated the supply and demand for officers. (Strictly speaking, the involuntary recall of reserve officers has borne much of the brunt of changing officer requirements, but this would also be the case in an all-volunteer force.) The training cost of $12,000 per officer for the officer candidate programs was used to estimate the variable training costs for officers shown in table A-X.

When the training and travel cost savings are subtracted from the incremental budget expenditures for military pay and allowances, the additional budget expenditures for the active duty all-volunteer force (excluding medical doctors and dentists) are estimated to be $1.92 billion per year in FY 1977 through 1979.

In order to sustain the reserve forces on an all-volunteer basis, it will be necessary to raise the reserve forces budget by $240 million. Other budget items (for the medical corps, additional recruiting expenses, establishment of proficiency pay for first-term enlisted men, etc.) add another $380 million. The total increment is, therefore, estimated to be $2.54 billion per year.

The implementation of the recommended basic pay rates and other items of compensation will result in an increase in federal income taxes paid by individuals in the active duty and reserve forces. These added taxes should properly be deducted in calculating the incremental budget expense of an all-volunteer force. For FY 1977 through 1979 they are estimated to be $420 million.

Thus the net additional budget expense required to maintain an all-volunteer force equivalent in strength to a 2.5 million man mixed force on a stable, continuing basis is about $2.12 billion per year. For the 2.0 million man force the comparable figure is $1.47 billion; for the 2.25 million man force it is $1.74 billion; and for the 3.0 million man force, $4.55 billion.

Smaller Forces

The military pay increases recommended by the Commission (which were used to calculate the military pay and allowances of the all-volunteer forces) would support active duty forces that are larger than the force strength objectives for forces of 2.25 and 2.0 million men even during the transition years FY 1973 through 1976. Our projections imply that if the recommended pay increases were put into effect, the services could raise mental qualification standards, thereby reducing the percentage of mental group IV enlistments below the 20 percent maximum assumed in the study. In fact, the projected flows of true volunteers imply that nearly all recruits could be drawn from the top three mental groups. On the other hand, if the Army continued to accept up to 20 percent mental group IV enlistments, our projections show that military pay levels could be reduced while meeting the strength objectives during the transition, for the 2.25 and 2.0 million man forces. The estimated Army recruitment deficits together with an elasticity of supply of 1.25 imply that the minimum increases in first-term pay needed

TABLE A–XII.—Reserve manpower expenditures [1]
[millions]

| | Unmodified FY 1977–79 stable reserve force | | |
	Draft	All-volunteer	Difference
2.00 Force			
Military pay and allowances .	$ 714.1	$ 834.2	$120.1
Personnel-related [2]	238.1	248.0	9.9
Total	952.2	1,082.2	130.0
2.25 Force			
Military pay and allowances .	792.4	927.7	135.3
Personnel-related [2]	241.7	267.9	26.2
Total	1,034.1	1,195.6	161.5
2.50 Force			
Military pay and allowances .	864.9	1,025.6	160.7
Personnel-related [2]	220.5	292.7	72.2
Total	1,085.4	1,318.3	232.9
3.00 Force			
Military pay and allowances .	898.7	1,193.5	294.8
Personnel-related [2]	127.9	282.8	154.9
Total	1,026.6	1,476.3	449.7

to maintain the 2.25 and 2.0 million men forces during the transition years were 24.4 and 11.8 percent respectively. If these lower pay levels had been adopted for all-volunteer forces of 2.25 and 2.0 million men (and the Commission *does not recommend* this), the military pay and allowances budget for enlisted men could have been reduced by $345 and $714 million below the figures shown in tables A-VIII and A-IX, respectively.

Maintaining Force Levels at Three Million Men

It was noted earlier that the recommended pay scales would *not* attract enough recruits to maintain an all-volunteer force of equivalent strength to a 3.0 million man mixed force. The data in table A-III indicate that the

TABLE A–XII.—Reserve manpower expenditures [1]
[millions] Continued

| | Modified FY 1977–79 stable reserve force | | |
	Draft	All-volunteer	Difference
2.00 Force			
Military pay and allowances .	$ 633.0	$ 744.2	$111.2
Personnel-related [2]	187.1	210.0	22.9
Total	820.1	954.2	134.1
2.25 Force			
Military pay and allowances .	701.6	826.3	124.7
Personnel-related [2]	184.4	224.9	40.5
Total	886.0	1,051.2	165.2
2.50 Force			
Military pay and allowances .	765.3	912.0	146.7
Personnel-related [2]	156.8	244.2	87.4
Total	922.1	1,156.2	234.1
3.00 Force			
Military pay and allowances .	792.4	1,060.7	268.3
Personnel-related [2]	59.8	231.5	171.7
Total	852.2	1,292.2	440.0

[1] Not offset for income taxes recovered.
[2] Training and travel; excludes military personnel costs.

overall deficit in enlisted force strengths would be only 3.8 percent in FY 1975. The deficits between target and sustainable force levels are, however, unevenly distributed, being largest, 25.0 percent, for the Army. To eliminate this deficit, first-term enlisted pay would have to be approximately 17 percent higher than the Commission has recommended in this report. The pay of career enlisted men and officers would also have to be advanced to prevent inversions in the pay profiles. When these higher rates of pay are applied to the estimated length of service distributions of enlisted men and officers, the military pay and allowances budget for an all-volunteer force is $5.0 billion higher than for the equivalent mixed force.

The summary of these budget estimates appears in table A-XI.

Reserve Forces Budgets

The estimated average annual manpower budgets for each of the four equally effective all-volunteer and mixed reserve forces for FY 1977 to 1979 are given in table A-XII. The mixed force estimates use 1970 compensation profiles, including the assumed 8.0 percent pay increase. Compensation for the three smaller all-volunteer reserve forces was computed using the Commission's recommended pay levels. Compensation for the largest reserve force is based on the pay levels required for the 3.0 million man all-volunteer active force.

Military and Civilian Compensation

Compensation comparisons, like those in tables 5-II and 5-III in chapter 5, always raise two kinds of questions: (1) has compensation been properly measured for the individuals being compared and (2) are the particular comparisons drawn, valid ones? These two questions are discussed below.

Measurement of Compensation

The civilian earnings figures used in this study are those generated by the Census Bureau's Current Population Survey (CPS), and are based on individual earnings reported to census interviewers. The value of employers' contributions to fringe benefits is derived from annual expenditure data for such benefits submitted by private firms to the U.S. Chamber of Commerce.

The military cash items of pay incorporated in the regular and total compensation figures are based on a random sample of pay records generated by each of the four services. Since these pay records show the actual cash payments to individuals, the estimates of military cash pay derived from them are probably superior to those generated by the Census Bureau. The value of items provided to military personnel in-kind has been derived from Department of Defense estimates and from other sources. In most instances, we have incorporated the lowest of the available estimates.

For instance, food provided in kind was valued at $1.32 per day; the Defense Department's estimate of the cost. That figure excludes the costs of preparation, service buildings, and equipment. Similarly, medical services have been valued at about $92 per person per year. This estimate is based on the costs of comprehensive medical insurance; costs which are significantly below those actually incurred (about $400 annually per individual for active military men, their dependents, and retired personnel). The current value of retired pay has been estimated by discounting future benefits at 10 percent per year, a discount rate significantly above the 3½ percent used by the Government. The higher discount rate greatly reduces the value of these benefits.

A conscious effort was made to use minimal estimates of income-in-kind, recognizing that the value of such items to the individual is likely on average to be lower than the costs of providing them. If there is any bias in our measurement of compensation, it is probably in the direction of underestimating military compensation for those in the latter stages of their careers.

With regard to the representative nature of the two measures of compensation, the average level of military pay for a given level of education and experience is probably more representative than is the average level of civilian pay. Even when age and education are held constant, the variability in pay among civilians is significantly greater than the variability in military pay.

Validity of the Comparisons

The question of the validity of our comparisons breaks down into three subquestions:

1. Are compensation comparisons by education and age or years of experience superior to compensation comparisons by occupation or by position? We have used the former because education and age or years of experience are objective characteristics that we can measure with reasonable accuracy; whereas de-

ciding what civilian position is comparable to op-
erating a submarine sonar or to firing a mortar is a
subjective exercise fraught with difficulties.

Also, the "job approach" focuses on the nature
of the position rather than the qualifications of the
individuals holding that position. Admittedly, education and experience are only two of the many
qualitative characteristics that determine pay. But
these two characteristics are among the most important ones and their market value is easily measured.
Moreover, we have used them to compare average
compensation for two similar groups, each of which
includes individuals who are both more and less
successful than those receiving the average level of
compensation for the group as a whole. By choosing
two qualities (formal education and on-the-job training or experience) which produce significant differences in civilian earnings, we are best able to
relate military pay to civilian alternatives which
influence career decisions.

The final and probably most important reason for
choosing these two qualitative characteristics has
been our recognition that individuals are only partly
influenced by how well they are remunerated for
their performance of a particular task or in a particular position. In choosing careers or employers,
they are also interested in advancement opportunities
or the speed of movement between jobs and levels
of responsibility. The education-experience classification highlights one's earnings opportunities throughout his entire career. The compensation profiles derived from this classification show the levels of pay
at a point in time as well as the changes in compensation over time. As such, they emphasize the
major dimensions that influence the individual's
career decision—the alternative levels of compensation over time in both military and civilian careers.

2. Is the quality of military personnel higher (or lower)
than that of the civilians with whom their compensation is being compared? More precisely, do
military selection procedures or self-selectivity result
in an average quality for military personnel exceed-

ing (or falling below) that of the civilian group to which they are compared? This is a very hard question to answer. It is difficult even to define "quality", much less determine whether it is higher or lower in the military than elsewhere. Fortunately, our comparisons center on only those aspects of quality which influence compensation. The fragmentary evidence on these aspects suggests no significant differences, if any, in the average level of quality between the groups being compared. On the one hand, the military services reject those with the lowest mental (AFQT) scores and those with physical handicaps at the initial entry point. On the other hand, a large number of those with high AFQT scores have been exempted from military service because they had either college student or occupational deferments. Also, upon completion of the initial term of service, the separations from the military have in the past tended to be proportionately greater among those of higher skills and levels of education than among those with lower skills and levels of education.

It has been argued that selectivity for promotion makes the quality of military personnel relatively superior. But, particular selective promotional steps occur in the later stages of a military career and do not become too critical until about the 20-years-of-service point.

The various factors mentioned above have probably prevented the emergence of significant differences in the average quality of the two groups. This conclusion is substantiated by the observed absence of any significant difference in civilian earnings between veterans and non-veterans of the same age and with the same educational levels. Indeed, the civilian earnings of retired service personnel are, on average, below those of civilians of like age and educational background.

Finally, we have attempted to compensate for any possible residual difference in quality favoring the military by comparing military compensation with the compensation for a group of civilians with higher levels of education than those of the military group.

For example, enlisted compensation was compared with civilian compensation for only white, male, high-school graduates. The enlisted ranks, however, contain a significant proportion of individuals (about 25 percent) who have not completed high school. Similarly, officer compensation was compared with the compensation for white males with 16 or more years of education, even though about 30 percent of the officer population are not college graduates.

3. Should the levels of military compensation equal the levels of compensation of equally qualified civilians? This issue involves the respective heights of the two compensation profiles—not their shapes or slopes.

While civilian high school or college graduates work in a variety of activities and under extremely divergent conditions, military personnel are likely to experience greater hazards and hardships in the service. For this reason, we are unable to claim that equality between military and civilian compensation represents true comparability. In fact, we suspect that higher levels of remuneration for military than for equally qualified civilian personnel will be necessary to achieve comparability in both monetary and non-monetary conditions of service. The excess of military over civilian compensation required will depend, among other things, on how many true volunteers the military will require.

APPENDIX C

Review of the 1966
Dept. of Defense Draft Study

A number of published and unpublished studies have developed estimates of the additional budget expenses that would be needed to move to an all-volunteer system. The estimates which have been most prominently reported in the press and Congress are those contained in the 1966 Department of Defense draft study.[1] The 1966 DOD study concluded that an all-volunteer force of 2.65 million men would add $4 billion to $17 billion per year to the defense budget. If the extreme estimates are excluded, the mid-range expenditure estimates are from $5 billion to $8 billion per year. The Department of Defense estimates are substantially higher than our estimate that an additional $2.12 billion per year will be needed to sustain an all-volunteer force of 2.5 million men on a stable basis.

A careful review of the 1966 DOD draft study was conducted to reconcile the differences in these estimates. The DOD study concluded that the unemployment rate in the civilian economy had a significant effect on both the demand for and supply of military personnel. Two alternative unemployment rates, 5.5 and 4.0 percent, were used in the DOD projections. In addition, three alternative estimates of the elasticity of supply (which describes the

---

[1] The text and supporting data of the DOD study appear in *Review of the Administration of the Selective Service System*. Hearings before the House Armed Services Committee, June 1966, pp. 9999–10174.

responsiveness of the supply of volunteers to changes in military pay) were examined for each assumed unemployment rate, thereby producing a total of six estimated budget increments. As we have noted earlier in appendix A, the unemployment variable was not statistically significant in our studies of first-term enlistments. Hence, we omitted unemployment as an explicit variable, and generated only a single set of projections.

At the outset, it is instructive to examine the six budget estimates which are reproduced in table C-I. The rows in table C-I present the annual increments (or decrements) to the defense manpower budget required to maintain an all-volunteer force under different assumptions. Table C-I reveals that between 92 and 95 percent of the added budget expense is due to the enlisted forces. Our review

TABLE C–I.—Estimated increase in payroll costs necessary to obtain an all-volunteer force of 2.7 million *
[billions]

	5.5-percent unemployment rate			4.0-percent unemployment rate		
	Low	Best	High	Low	Best	High
Enlisted:						
Increase in active-duty pay	$3.57	$5.02	$ 8.96	$5.21	$7.64	$14.61
Increase in future retirement benefits.	.16	.39	1.03	.42	.79	1.94
Savings from reduced turnover	—.35	—.41	—.54	—.41	—.51	—.72
Total	3.38	5.0	9.45	5.22	7.92	15.83
Officers' total	.29	.42	.83	.29	.42	.83
Grand total .	3.67	5.42	10.28	5.51	8.34	16.66

* "Review of the Administration and Operation of the Selective Service System," *Hearings before the Committee on Armed Services, House of Representatives*, 89th Cong., 2d sess., June 1966, pp. 10042–10043.

will be limited to the estimated added budget expenses for the enlisted force.

The relative increase in pay, (M_1/M_0) that is needed to maintain an all-volunteer force of 2.65 million men depends on three factors: (1) the supply of true volunteers assuming the draft is ended with no accompanying change in military pay; (2) the number of accessions that are needed to meet the prescribed force strength objectives; and (3) the elasticity of supply. The budget estimates in the Commission study reported in appendix A also involved assumptions about these three factors. In what follows, we point out the major differences in assumptions between the 1966 DOD draft study and the Commission study and indicate how these differences account for the widely divergent budget estimates.

Supply of True Volunteers in the Absence of a Draft

The 1966 DOD study dealt with projections for the period FY 1970 through 1971, while the Commission study related to a steady state in the period FY 1977 to 1979. The estimated annual flows of true volunteers for enlisted ranks taken from the DOD study are presented in the top panel of table C-II. For comparative purposes, our estimates of the supply of true volunteers with no draft and no pay change are shown in the last column. The male population in the 17-20 year-old range is projected to be 7,555,000 for the FY 1970 through 1971 period as compared to 8,589,000 for the FY 1977 through 1979 period. To adjust for this approximately 14 percent increase in the pool of potential recruits, the voluntary enlistments were converted to enlistment rates appearing in the second panel of table C-II.

The true voluntary enlistment rates were not appreciably different in the two studies. In fact, the Army enlistment rate used in the Commission study lies mid-way between the two Army enlistment rates reported in the 1966 DOD study. This result is not surprising since both the DOD and Commission studies estimated the incidence of draft-motivated volunteers by analyzing the same survey of first-term enlisted men conducted in the Fall of 1964.

TABLE C–II.—Supply of true volunteers in the absence of a draft

	1966 DOD draft study		Commission study
	percent unemployment		
	5.5	4.0	
Number of true volunteers per year			
All Services ..	317	272	312
Army	106	91	110
Voluntary enlistment rates [a] (percent)			
All Services ..	4.20	3.60	3.63
Army	1.40	1.20	1.29
Required accessions			
All Services ..	500	512	342
Army	220	232	148
Recruitment deficits [b]			
All Services ..	1.58	1.88	1.10
Army	2.08	2.55	1.34
Annual turnover rate [c] (percent)			
All Services ..	21.3	21.8	16.4
Army	25.3	26.4	17.9

[a] The 17–20 year old male population, FY 1970–71, was 7,555 thousand, and for FY 1977–79 8,589 thousand. The enlistment rates are expressed as percentages.

[b] The recruitment deficit is defined as the ratio of required accessions to the supply of true volunteers appearing in the first panel. A ratio of 1.58 means a 58-percent shortfall in volunteers that must be met by increasing the supply of volunteers through higher pay.

[c] The annual personnel turnover rate is simply the number of required accessions expressed as a percentage of active duty force strength. In the DOD study, the total enlisted force was approximately 2.35 million men with an Army of roughly 870 thousand men. The enlisted force for the 2.5 million men force in the Commission study was 2,089 thousand with an Army of 827 thousand.

Required Accessions

In the Commission study, estimates of the accessions required to maintain enlisted force strength objectives were based on loss rates in the pre-Vietnam period. The improvements in retention which result from having only true volunteers and from higher levels of military pay were incorporated into the Commission's projection model. Hence, the annual turnover rate of Army enlisted men was projected to decline from 25 percent in the mixed force to 18 percent in the all-volunteer forces.

The assumptions which were used in the 1966 DOD study could not be found. However, the implications of their procedures are summarized in the last panel of table C-II, which shows the implied annual turnover rates. The required Army accessions in the DOD study imply annual turnover rates of 25 and 26 percent respectively, which are approximately the rates obtained for mixed forces of draftees and volunteers. We shall comment later on the importance of this estimate.

Elasticity of Supply

The elasticity of supply, B, is defined as the relative increase in voluntary enlistments resulting from a given relative increase in the ratio of military to civilian pay. In the Commission study, it was estimated that the elasticity of supply of voluntary enlistments was approximately 1.25, and this value was used in the projections. The 1966 DOD study assumed a supply function in which the elasticity declines as larger fractions of the available population are recruited into the Armed Forces. Given the relative recruitment deficits appearing in the fourth panel of table C-II, the elasticities implied by the first-term pay increases proposed in the 1966 DOD study can be calculated from the following equation:

$$\log (E_1/E_0) = B [\log (M_1/M_0)],$$

where the Army recruitment deficits are used as the pertinent shortfalls. The relative pay increase and relative

Army recruitment deficit for the six cases identified by the 1966 DOD study are shown in table C-III. The implied elasticities, B, are found to vary between 0.7 and 1.25. Thus, the elasticity estimate used in the Commission study lies at the upper extreme of the elasticities assumed in the DOD study. Finally, the level of first-term pay M_1 implied by the pay increases is shown in the second column of table C-III. The first-term pay of enlisted men, M_0 which prevailed in 1965 was reported in the DOD study as follows: The low estimate of first-term pay for enlisted men required to maintain a voluntary force is $6,147 in 1965 prices, while the high estimate is $13,045.

TABLE C–III.—Implied first-term pay and elasticity of supply for the DOD study

	Relative increase in first-term pay M_1/M_0	Annual first-term pay M_1	Army recruitment deficit E_1/E_0	Implied elasticity B
5.5-percent un-employment				
Low	1.80	$ 6,147	2.08	1.26
Best	2.11	7,206	2.08	.98
High	2.81	9,596	2.08	.71
4.0-percent un-employment				
Low	2.14	7,308	2.55	1.23
Best	2.63	8,981	2.55	.97
High	3.82	13,045	2.55	.70

Sensitivity of Budget Estimates to Estimates of Requirements and Elasticities

The widely divergent estimates of the additional budget expenditures for an all-volunteer force ($4 billion to $17 billion in the 1966 DOD study and about $2 billion in the Commission study) can be explained by the differences in the respective estimates of requirements and elasticities. The 1966 DOD study concluded that pay for first-term enlisted men would have to rise by 80 to 282 percent to attract a sufficient flow of true volunteers. (See table C-IV for 1965 pay rates.) The estimated relative pay increases (M_1/M_0) depends critically on the estimated recruitment shortfall (E_1/E_0) and the elasticity of supply, B.

In order to show how these variables are related we calculated the pay increases (M_1/M_0) necessary to achieve an all-volunteer force for alternative values of (E_1/E_0) and B. These are shown in the top panel of table C-V. The lower panel of table C-V shows what the approximate 1966 DOD budget increments would have been *if* the DOD study had used the particular recruitment deficit shown in the column heading and elasticity estimate shown for the row heading. For example, if the DOD study had arrived at an estimated elasticity of 1.0 and a recruitment deficit of 1.74, their procedures would have generated an aprpoximate budget increase of $3.33 billion. The data of table C-V enable us to explain why the two studies arrived at such widely different estimates.

TABLE C–IV.—**Military pay of first-term enlisted men—1965 pay rates**

Years of service	Tax equivalent income	Supplements	Total military income
0 to 1	$1,830	$ 582	$2,412
1 to 2	2,143	788	2,931
2 to 3	2,991	950	3,941
3 to 4	3,344	1,034	4,378
Average	2,577	839	3,415

The relative recruitment deficits (E_1/E_0) is the ratio of required accessions, E_1, to the supply of true volunteers in the absence of a draft with no pay changes E_0. As indicated above, there is little disagreement in the two studies on the true voluntary enlistment rates. However, the projection period for the Commission study, FY 1977 through 1979, is characterized by a population pool that is some 14 percent larger than the population pool for the FY 1970 through 1971 period of the DOD projections. This fact alone operates to reduce the recruitment deficit.

TABLE C–V.—Relative increase in military pay
(M_1/M_0) and DOD budget expenses *
[for alternative elasticities and recruitment deficits]

Elasticity of supply B	Relative recruitment deficit (E_1/E_0) ** (percent turnover)				
	1.57 (18%)	1.74 (20%)	1.91 (22%)	20.9 (24%)	2.26 (26%)
Relative increase in first-term pay (M_1/M_0)					
0.700	1.91	2.21	2.52	2.84	3.21
0.850	1.70	1.91	2.14	2.38	2.61
1.000	1.57	1.74	1.91	2.09	2.26
1.125	1.49	1.64	1.78	1.93	2.06
1.250	1.44	1.56	1.68	1.80	1.92
1.375	1.38	1.50	1.60	1.71	1.81
Approximate budget expense of all-volunteer force (billions)					
0.700	$4.29	$5.91	$7.71	$10.47	$12.81
0.850	3.11	4.29	5.51	6.90	8.23
1.000	2.37	3.33	4.29	5.31	6.20
1.125	1.92	2.77	3.56	4.40	5.14
1.250	1.64	2.31	2.99	3.67	4.35
1.375	1.30	1.98	2.54	3.16	3.73

* The approximate annual increase in budget expenditures for the all-volunteer force of 2.65 million men was calculated by linear interpolation of the budget increases reported in the 1966 DOD draft study as shown in the last line of table C-I. The recruitment deficits that were used in the 1966 DOD study were 2.08 for an unemployment rate of 5.5 percent and 2.55 for an unemployment rate of 4.0 percent.

** The numbers in parentheses indicate the annual turnover rate for Army enlisted men which would have generated these relative recruitment deficits. Hence, a turnover rate of 20 percent would have produced a recruitment deficit of 1.74.

The estimated required accessions for the Army, E_1, were, however, very different. The 1966 estimates imply that if all recruits were true volunteers who enlisted for three-year terms, the Army would experience an annual turnover rate of 25 to 26 percent. In the period FY 1957 to 1965 when nearly half of all Army accessions were two-year draftees, the annual turnover rate of Army enlisted men was between 20 and 25 percent. It is now nearly 34 percent because fully two-thirds of all Army accessions are draftees. In the 1966 DOD study, it was assumed that the draft would be continued to June 30, 1969. Hence, the DOD projection period FY 1970 to 1971 applied to a transition period in which force strengths remained stable. No statement is made in the DOD study to indicate when the pay of enlisted men would be advanced. If it had been raised in 1966, the greater retention of an all-volunteer force would have occurred by 1970. On the other hand, if pay were advanced on July 1, 1969, some improvement in retention would still have taken place especially when pay rates were more than doubled for first-term enlisted men and increased by at least 50 percent for second-term enlisted men. We believe that the DOD estimates of required accessions are unreasonably high. If the 1966 DOD study had used an annual turnover rate of 20 percent, the added budget expenditure for an all-volunteer force would have varied between $2.31 billion (for an elasticity of 1.25) and $5.91 billion (for an elasticity of 0.7). The implications of additional budget expenditures of $2 billion to $6 billion a year are, indeed, very different from estimates of $4 billion to $17 billion.

Finally, a considerable part of the added budget expenditures arises because of pay increases to the career enlisted force. If first-term pay must be doubled from $3,415 to $6,830 per year, the pay of the career force must also be raised. These career pay increases should lead to significantly higher re-enlistment rates which, in turn, would reduce personnel turnover. The Commission study incorporated these effects in generating estimates of personnel turnover rates. Moreover, the recommended pay increase in the Commission study led to only modest increases in the pay of career enlisted men. Although the 1966 DOD study provided higher career pay to prevent inversions in the enlisted pay structure (enlisted men with 1 to 3 years of service earning more than men with 6 to 12 years of service), they do not mention pay comparisons between enlisted men and officers. The high budget estimate of $17 billion implied that a new recruit would receive annual military pay of $13,045—considerably more than the pay of newly commissioned officers.

INDEX

Index